THE VOYAGE OF LIFE

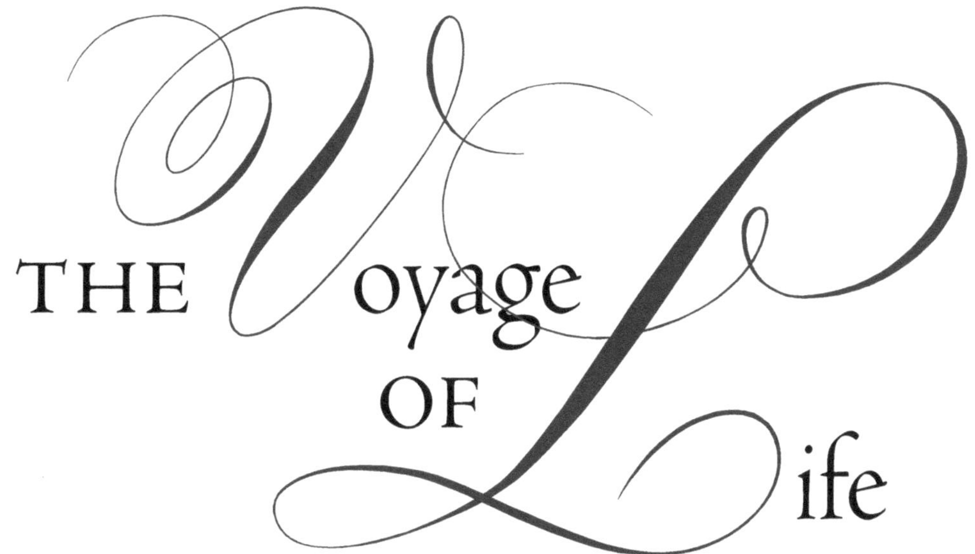

THE Voyage OF Life

The Sacred Vision of Thomas Cole

BY ADDISON HODGES HART

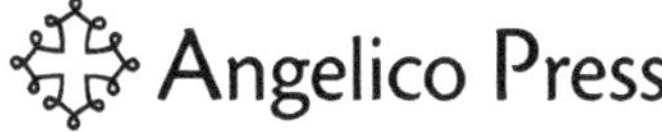

First published in the USA
by Angelico Press 2023

For information, address:
Angelico Press, Ltd.
169 Monitor St.
Brooklyn, NY 11222
www.angelicopress.com

pb: 978-1-62138-914-9
cloth: 978-1-62138-915-6

Book and cover design
by Michael Schrauzer

In grateful memory of
Jim Forest,
Writer, Peacemaker, Activist, Friend

Contents

ACKNOWLEDGEMENT

All selections from Thomas Cole's poems in this book are taken from *Thomas Cole's Poetry*, compiled by Marshall B. Tymn and published by George Shumway Publisher, Inc. (3900 Deep Run Lane, York, PA 17406). The author and publisher wish to thank Dorothy Shumway for graciously granting us permission to reprint from this — the only — collection of Cole's poetry.

By mortal man that River of dark source
Is named the "Stream of Life"; with constant flow
With many a winding on its downward course,
At times it lags along with motion slow,
At times impetuous o'er the rocky steep
It journeyeth onward toward The Eternal Deep.

There in that vast Profound — that darkest Dread
That Silence — that immeasurable Gloom,
The Breathless — Shoreless — the Un-islanded
Of the great World — of mighty Time the Tomb
It sinks, it vanishes and mortal eye
Perplexed and troubled, trembling turns on high.

Thomas Cole, *The Voyage of Life*

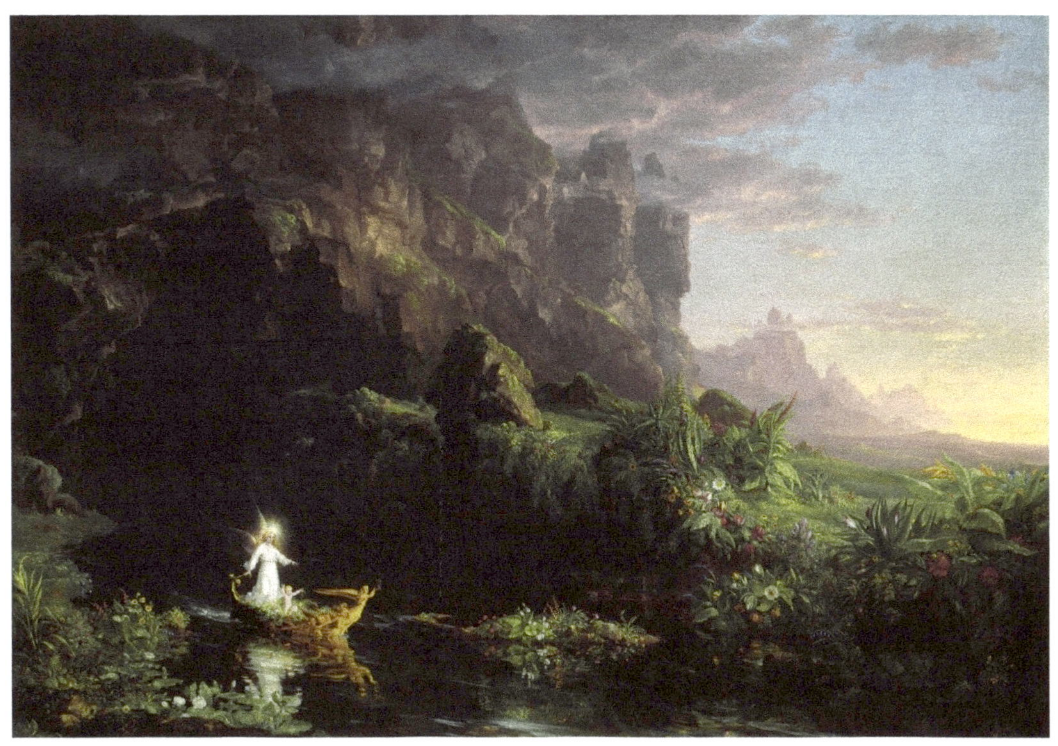

FIRST SCENE: "CHILDHOOD"

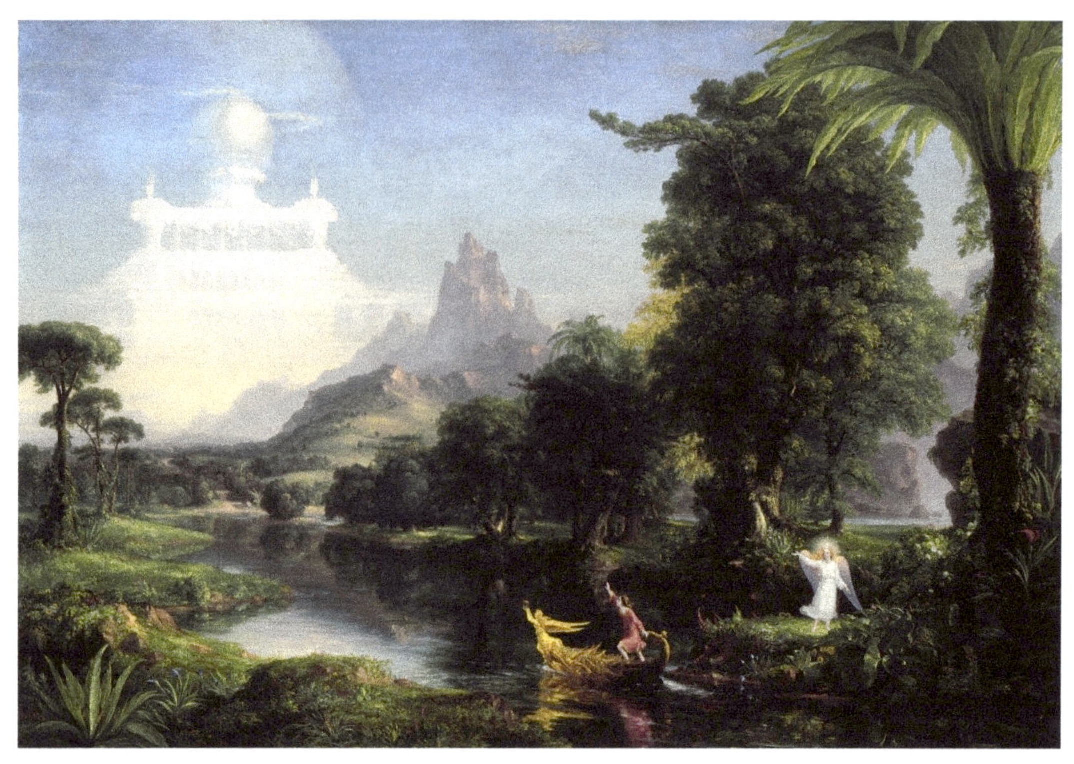

SECOND SCENE: "YOUTH"

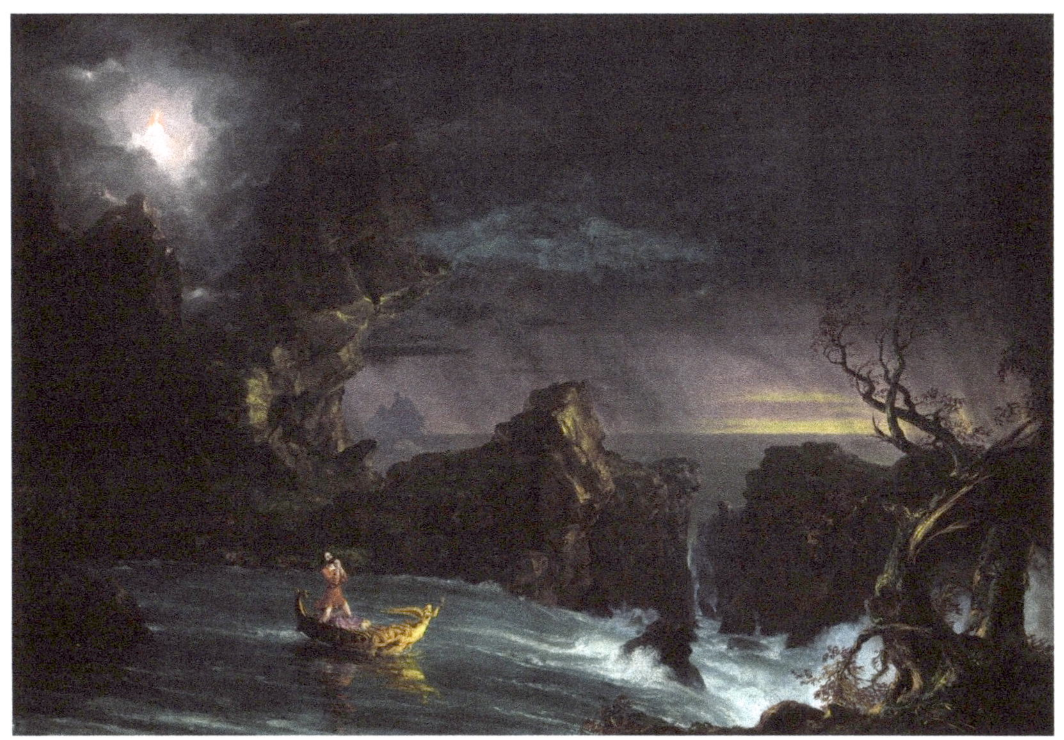

THIRD SCENE: "MANHOOD"

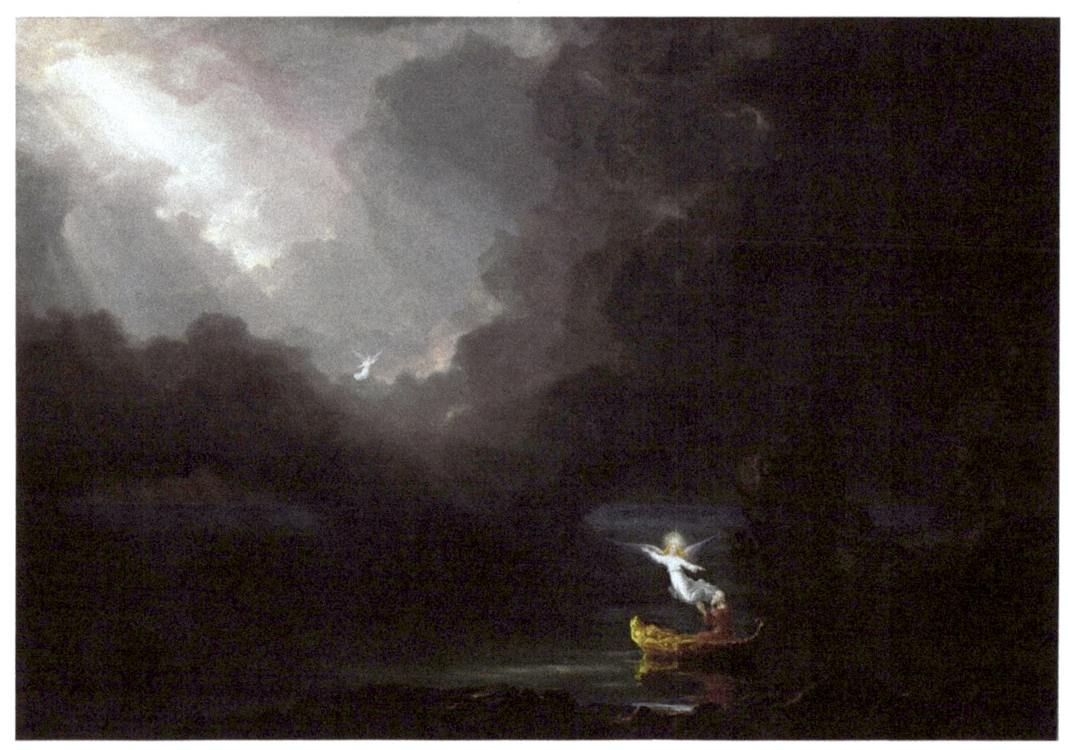

FOURTH SCENE: "OLD AGE"

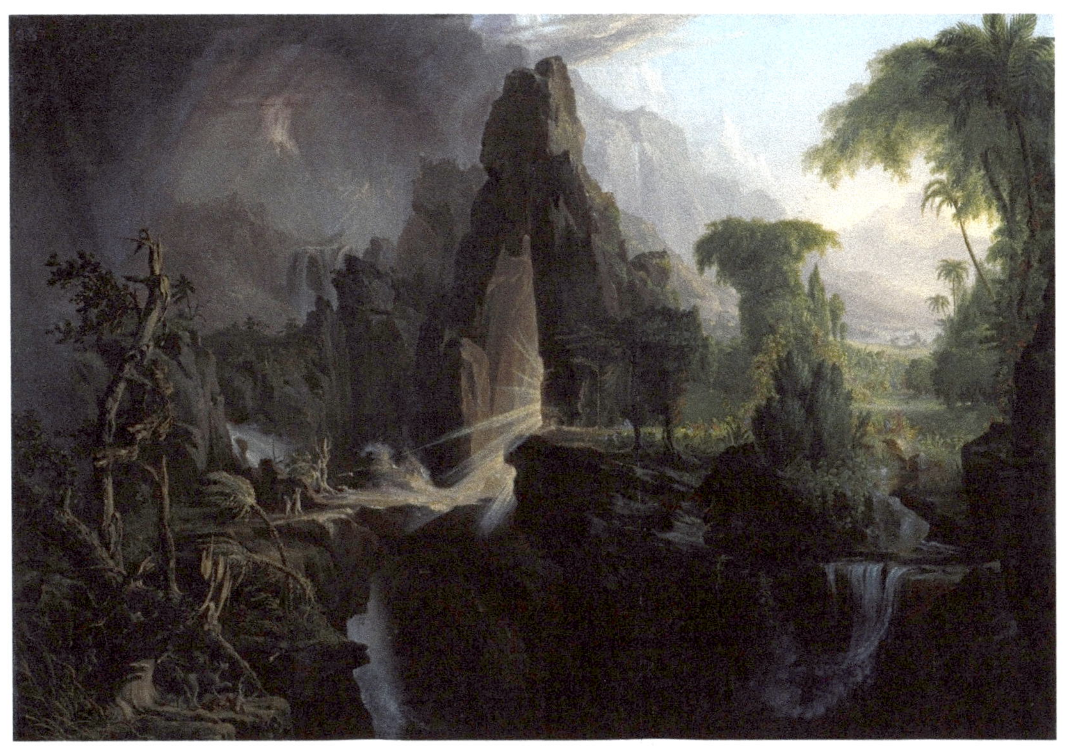

"THE EXPULSION FROM THE GARDEN OF EDEN"

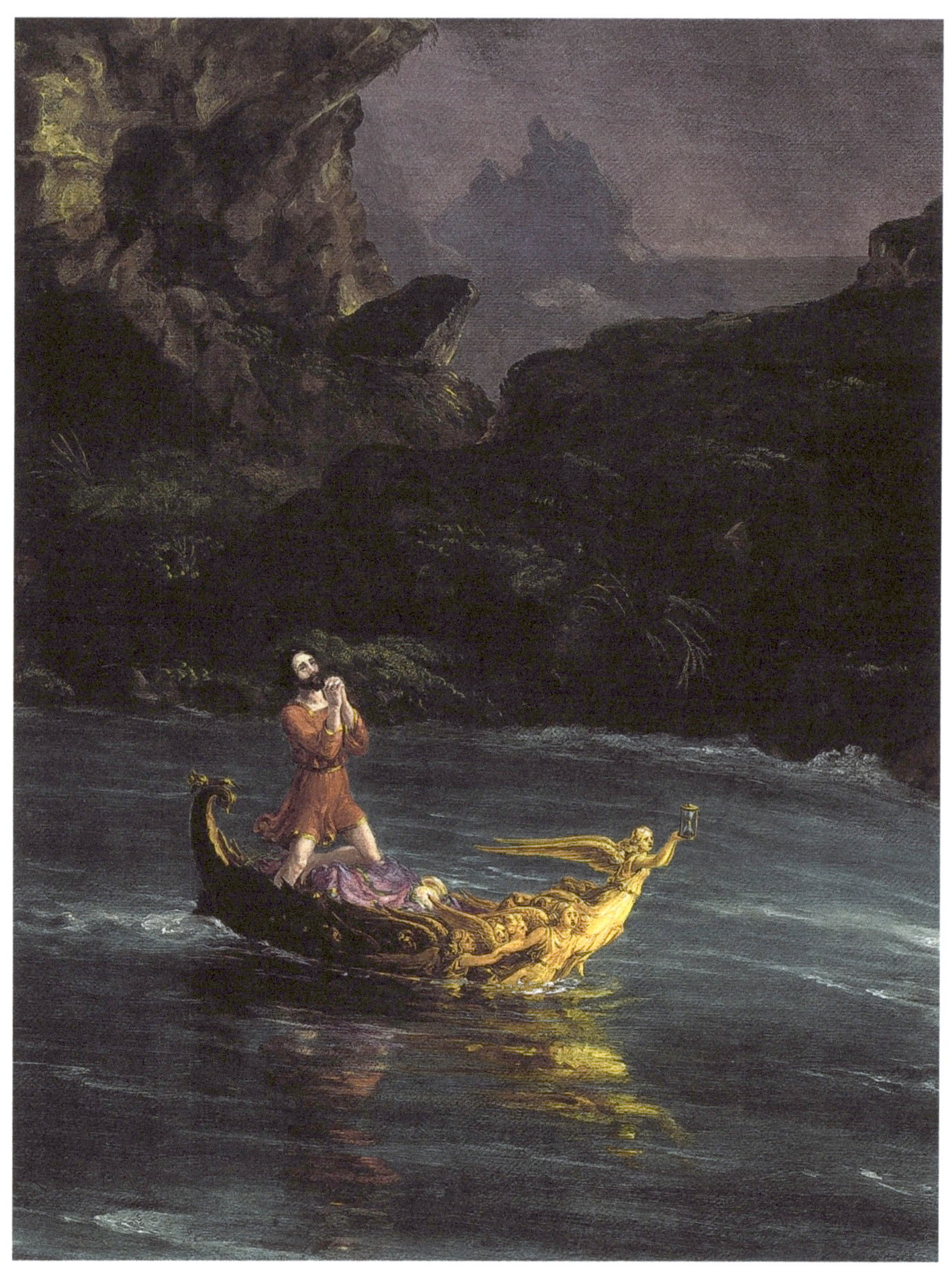

"MANHOOD," DETAIL

I. The Soul in Transit

"We are born in mystery, we live in mystery, and we die in mystery."
(Huston Smith)

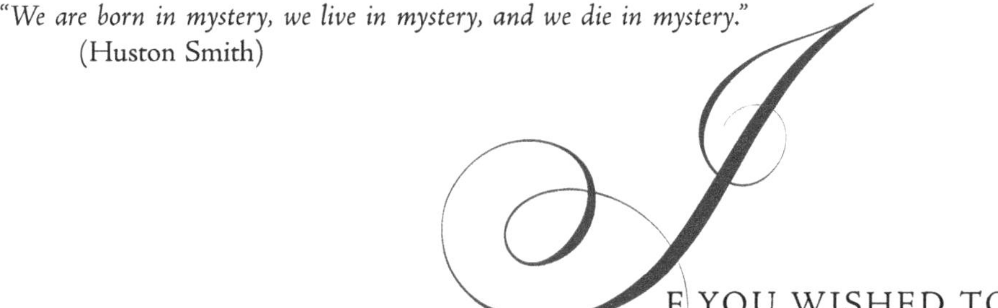

IF YOU WISHED TO portray in art the journey of human life, from birth to death, how might you go about it? How would you imagine it? Put differently, if you were to attempt to depict allegorically both the brevity and vicissitudes of human existence as all of us experience it, so that any viewer of your work might see himself or herself in it, how might you realize it? How might you display in a work or several works of art, in a way that connects intimately with an observer, the growing awareness each of us gains over time of impermanence, that of ourselves and likewise of everyone and everything else besides, or the perennial human longing for the ineffable, for God or eternity, so that these might be rendered inventively? Each human life embraces hopes, fears, dependence, desire for independence, struggles of many kinds, vulnerability, failure, the inevitability of death... But how could all this be represented in paint on canvas? What metaphors would you use, what imagery to convey these things? How might you go about creating such an impressive work, rendering the theme's philosophical, psychological, and spiritual complexities so plainly that the meaning could not be missed, even by the inexperienced and the young?

This was the aim that the American Romantic artist Thomas Cole—later regarded as the founder of what would be called the Hudson River School of artists—set for himself in *The Voyage of Life*. Some years before he managed to obtain a commission to paint it, he conceived the idea of a series of four large paintings, each showing a different stage of a single representative life. He began work on the project in 1839, and despite the daunting nature of the enterprise, Cole believed both that his entire vision for the series could be realized and that its meaning could be made plain to viewers. "The subject is an allegorical one," he wrote in a letter, "but *perfectly intelligible . . .*"[1] He was confident in his abilities by this time in his life, but he had no illusions that it would prove a simple task. It wasn't like composing a poem, he noted, which might be jotted down with a bit of inspiration and finished with relatively small effort. Cole wrote to Samuel Ward, the patron who eventually commissioned the series (and would die unexpectedly that same year) to this effect: "The poetical conception of a subject may not be difficult, for it is spontaneous; but to imagine that which is to be embodied in light, and shadow, and colour—that which is strictly pictorial—is an accumulative work of the mind."[2] And what he proposed to create was no less than a series of truly monumental paintings. He had successfully achieved something of a similarly large-scale nature before—a series of five sizeable, richly detailed paintings entitled *The Course of Empire* (1831–1836). In that project, he had tackled the rise and fall of civilizations—collective humanity—in powerful, unsettling detail. With this new series, he hoped to express something analogous about the progress of the solitary human soul.

One has the impression that the governing image of a long and winding river as an allegory for the course of time had, perhaps, suggested itself to him gradually; possibly his excursions along the Genesee River influenced the conception.[3] The Romantics looked to nature for inspiration. In Europe, they could look both to nature and to the remains of the classical and medieval past, but in America, unadorned nature alone provided what the Romantic soul needed to awaken the imagination—although even in Cole's day, nature was already in retreat before the inroads of civilization (something Cole often commented upon and lamented). Nature, as the Romantics saw it, was the supreme muse and a revelation of God. One could discover life's greatest truths in it—and the grim revelations of blight, decay, and death as well. All of these would appear in Cole's grand design. The guiding image for the series would be a river, an appropriate age-old symbol, from Heraclitus to Isaac Watts, for time's flow, impermanence, and the passage of life. All the other imagery in the four paintings would have it as their governing context.

1 Louis Legrand Noble, *The Life and Works of Thomas Cole*, ed. Elliot S. Vesell (Hensonville: Black Dome Press Corp., 1997), 203. Emphasis added.

2 Ibid., 205.

3 In the words of Louis Legrand Noble, *The Voyage of Life* "exhibits here and there, in the sweet windings of its stream, in its alternately rapid and placid current, in the fine verdure of its banks and groves, and in its delightful atmospheric effects, the influence [of the Genesee River] upon his mind and feelings . . ." Noble, *Life and Works*, 205.

The other allegorical images would be a human figure in a boat, an angel, and the changing natural landscape about them. The last feature would shift from one painting to the next, from the verdant and Edenic to the terrors of the sublime, and finally to the immeasurable expanse of ocean calm. The vegetation lush or sparse, the skies clouded or clear, the rocks and crags and rapids would all add to the character—and hence the meaning—of each scene. And each scene would mirror the inner state of the figure in the boat. This use of vividly rendered natural scenery to reflect the interior condition at different stages of individual human development would work powerfully on the viewer. In fact, looking at the realized series even today, it gets under our skin, past our rational responses, and hits us at the level of imagination and emotion. We know it conveys truth, even that it is somewhat "didactic" in the best sense, but it isn't presented to us in speech or a system of thought or philosophy (as an interpretation, Cole would later compose a poem—but note, not a treatise or a series of bland notes). Of course, this is precisely what great art and literature—poetry or prose—is meant to do for us.

The series is about the individual soul. If *The Course of Empire* depicted human society in its rise and decline, *The Voyage of Life* depicts the solitary person in his trials and tribulations. As we will see, it doesn't present the viewer with an ideal figure, but with fluctuating, unpredictable, trouble-prone human life as we all know and experience it. Hence it touches us who see it as individuals, as persons, who are in numerous ways destined to be isolated from even our closest confidants at the loneliest core of ourselves. We know—or else we should know—that there are aspects of our inner life, our consciousness as we alone experience it, that we cannot impart to others. We are fated to be "self-centered" (which is not the same thing as selfish) simply because, as Paul Tillich wrote somewhere, we can only operate from the context of our own subjective centers. And yet, despite that fact, if we can look closely into our own solitary "center," we discover that, paradoxically, we have in common with all others that same shared condition of inner isolation. Cole may not have thought in these terms, but he captures nonetheless this aspect of our existence in his brilliant series of scenes. He could do so because, as his biography suggests again and again, he was a peculiarly sensitive and contemplative man. He could, in fact, look deeply into the world of nature outside himself and, at the same time, observe profoundly his own and everyone else's human nature and draw the proper analogy.

My appreciation of this series of paintings has been with me for most of my life. I cannot recall precisely the first time I laid eyes on these four grand canvases.[4] I know I was young, not yet eight, and the period was the early 1960s. The series was situated in its own room at the National Gallery in Washington DC (and, I believe, it still is).[5] Each of its four scenes dominated one of the room's four walls. Although I can't recall details of that first encounter, I do know that the paintings enthralled me from the outset. Today I live in Europe, and I haven't been able to visit them in well over a decade; but even in my adulthood, whenever I visited the Gallery, I made my pilgrim's way to them. In those early years, in that four-cornered room where they alone held sway, they took firm hold of my imagination. They fascinated me. It was obvious that the four scenes told a single story, and I knew, even as a small boy, that the story they told was true. Not factual, mind you, but true; children learn early to know the difference, even if they can't articulate what that is. I understood that the story included me somehow, that I was like that naïve, then confident, then desperate, then resigned aging figure in the boat. I grasped instantly what the story meant. Nobody needed to explain the allegory to me and something in me responded to it with an intuitive assent. In short, these scenes were, as Cole had said, "perfectly intelligible," even to someone of the single-digit age I was at the time.

In contrast to my early intuitive appreciation, however, it's a depressing fact that for some otherwise insightful art critics, the (for me all-important) feature of intelligibility seems to work against their opinion of Cole's art. One of the more inscrutable criticisms leveled at *The Voyage of Life* has been that the series lacks subtlety, that its symbolism is much too obvious, much too moralistic. To take a single but significant example, the late art historian Robert Hughes wrote of it that "to a modern eye, [the paintings] are unalloyed Victorian kitsch" (this despite the fact that the "Victorian" era had scarcely commenced when the series was conceived).[6] The implication of Hughes's superficial dismissal seems to be that Cole wears his heart too much on his sleeve, that the work is (in his opinion) sentimental and hence shallow, and that we — at least, "we art critics" of a certain sophistication — are much too urbane a breed to hold such stuff in esteem. Hughes had to admit, however, that *The Voyage of Life* was "the most popular series Cole produced" and that "nearly half a million

---

4 The recorded dimensions of the four original paintings, in order from Childhood to Old Age, are: 52 in. by 78 in., 53 in. by 76 in., 52.3 in. by 78 in., and 52.5 in. by 77.2 in.

5 What is exhibited in the National Gallery is, in fact, a duplicate series that Cole painted in Rome. Cole's original series is today housed in Utica, New York, at the Munson-Williams-Procter Arts Institute.

6 Robert Hughes, *American Visions: The Epic History of Art in America* (New York: Alfred A. Knopf, 1997), 150.

Americans flocked to see [it] in a memorial exhibition of Cole's work in 1848, and engravings made after the four paintings were once . . . a fixture of American parlors . . ."[7] Of course, for a modern art critic to say that a work of art was once actually *popular* during the Victorian age is to damn it with the faintest of faint praise, insinuating that it's fit only for middle-brow tastes or worse. The best that might be expected from that rarefied viewpoint is that, in quality, it's a few steps above a portrait of Elvis on black velvet.

It should be evident already that I disagree strongly with that kind of dismissive declaration, even when it comes from such a renowned critic as Robert Hughes. Frankly, it's worthless as criticism because it provides no criticism at all, substantial or otherwise. Despite my otherwise positive regard for him when he actually employed his considerable art-critical faculties, all Hughes presents us with in this instance is his thinly veiled bias. One looks in vain for anything more. His assessment isn't even minimally interesting—and certainly nowhere near as interesting as Cole's four vibrant and evocative scenes. Despite Hughes's appraisal, what makes *The Voyage of Life* appealing even to this day, and why "half a million Americans flocked to see" it back in 1848, and why it became for a long time "a fixture of American parlors," is primarily due to its undeniable intelligibility, matched by its stunning and evocative visual power. People from all backgrounds, all levels of education, and all income brackets can readily understand it (not to give in to caricature, but it does seem that popularity is the *bête noire* for a certain type of art connoisseur). It connects directly with the viewer even though the theme it presents is nothing less than the complexity of human life itself.

If then Cole is judged (as he should be) for achieving precisely what he set out to do, there can be no room for doubt that he succeeded admirably, and that the series is a masterwork of beautifully intelligible allegory.[8]

---

7 Ibid.

8 The one caveat I will make here is that when I say "everyone" can appreciate Cole's meaning based on our common human experience, it is a simplification and a generalization. Obviously, there are many whose lives have been marred at an early age, or who have endured hard struggles and real torments in childhood, or who have never entertained dreams for a happy future because their present was such a living nightmare, or who have died in the prime of life, and so on. Without ignoring such sufferings and the fact that misery attends our condition in many forms that Cole's work doesn't envisage, nonetheless we can recognize in it a general pattern of life's typical stages. I can't think of a culture anywhere in which the overall symbolism in these paintings would prove to be indecipherable.

Cole described *The Voyage of Life*, as we noted above, as "an accumulative work of the mind." In other words, the work grew incrementally in conception. It seems that what began as a fairly simple idea (a visibly aging figure in a boat on a river) increased in the richness of its detail as he went along, with additional features becoming definite and fixed in his mind—so much so that it now seems impossible to separate any of the features making up each scene as insignificant. All the details, however minute, exist together organically. Each scene is an accomplished whole, each part necessary to the overall effect of the completed series. There are, as well, common aspects that recur throughout the series, but changing or shifting from one scene to the next as the series progresses. Of these recurring features, I count six that are essential to every one of the four scenes. They are as follows:

First, there is at the very center of each scene what I refer to in this book as *the Soul*, by which I mean the child/youth/man/old man in the vessel. I refer to this central figure as "the Soul," rather than as "the man," because I believe this evolving image is intended to be an inclusive, not exclusive, symbol for the individual human being. He isn't strictly a male, in other words, any more than the Angel in the same scene is strictly a female. By "Soul," too, I mean not simply some immaterial essence situated "inside" each person, although Cole was a dualist who saw the soul as a sort of detachable entity enshrouded by the "clay" of the mortal body.[9] Rather, I use it as designating a personal life taken as an integrated whole. The word "Soul," then, includes the body, the senses, the mind, and so on—the full aggregation of properties.

Despite the choice of the figure's sex (which is hardly surprising, given the provenance of the paintings), there is nothing particularly "masculine" about him. We see him first as a child, then as an ambitious youth, then as a struggling middle-aged man imploring divine aid, and finally as an old man succumbing to death. There is nothing illustrative of swagger or "aggressiveness" in his appearance in any of the scenes. He is shown acting self-confidently only once in the series, and—suggestively—it is while making a serious error of judgment. At the same time, we see feminine figures surrounding him. The boat, in which the Soul travels, has carved figures of the Hours on it. The Hours were goddesses of the seasons, justice, order, and peace in Greek mythology. As I will note immediately below, this boat is in fact an extension of the Soul

9 This becomes evident in Cole's poetic explication of the final scene, "Old Age." See my comments on the topic in the last chapter.

(as is much else in the paintings). The vessel is one with him throughout, never absent, his emblematic complement. Its décor and its loss of features from scene to scene, the result of the battering it takes, fittingly symbolizes the wear and tear time takes on the Soul it carries. Likewise, the Angel who is present in every scene is unquestionably feminine in appearance and, as we shall see, in some sense united to him.

Second, then, there is *the boat,* which looks as if it is made of gold. As already mentioned, it serves as an extension of the Soul. It bears the images of the "winged Hours" (as Cole refers to them in the poem based on the series that he later wrote), indicating the swift movement of his life on the river of time.

The boat is a curious one for another reason: it lacks a mast and sail and has neither oars nor poles. It can neither be propelled nor effectively maneuvered by its passenger. All it has is a rudder, which first the Angel and then the youth use to steer the craft, but even that little bit of control is lost by the third scene of the series. In other words, the boat is entirely at the mercy of the current, which is its only driving force. There is no chance of its being rowed against the stream; the flowing river represents the relentless one-way directionality of time itself. The rudder—for as long as it lasts—merely assists in guiding the vessel, but ultimately it proves much too vulnerable for the unruly forces of nature. Cole is clearly indicating that time is inexorable and that our lives are never fully under our own, feeble control. Unforeseen difficulties, old age, and death await all those who live a full life. (I note in passing here that Cole himself did not live to see old age.)

The third essential feature in the paintings is *the Angel.* If the boat might be said to be an extension of the soul, the same can be postulated of the Angel. Throughout the painted scenes, this being appears as a source of light. In the poem Cole later composed, which interprets the series, the Angel is described in these terms:

> Radiant it stood and o'er its glorious head
> A star hung tremulous and brighter did appear
> Than Venus when the morn from cloud and mist is clear.[10]

The star above the Angel's head suggests intellect. By "intellect" I do not mean mere "brainpower," but rather the "higher" aspect of the soul, that which apprehends the spiritual or transcendent, that has the capacity to comprehend

10 Marshall B. Tymn, ed., *Thomas Cole's Poetry* (York: Liberty Cap Books, 1972), 146.

the whole. The Angel always has full oversight of the situation, even when the Soul in the boat has lost his way and his ability to steer his craft. She can be viewed both as a separate heavenly creature and, simultaneously, as the angelic aspect of human nature, which sees all things as interconnected and leading to an appointed end. She is Wisdom or Sophia, perhaps, the semi-divine intermediary between God and human beings referred to in the biblical wisdom books—both one with God and one with the deepest nature of the individual Soul.

Cole in his poem refers to the Angel as "it" as well as "she." I will refer to her consistently as "she" in this book, mainly to counterbalance the masculine pronoun for the voyaging Soul. If, as I surmise, the Angel is in some poetic sense the Soul's highest spiritual faculties and aspirations, as well as a separate entity in the paintings, it might not be too much of a stretch to suggest that she is a reminder of Jesus's saying that "in the resurrection" human beings "will be like the angels in heaven" (Matthew 22:30; Mark 12:25; Luke 20:35-36). Perhaps significantly, in the same year that the paintings were completed, the 41-year-old Cole was baptized in the Episcopal Church. It's just feasible that some idea of this sort might have crossed his mind. Be that as it may, his intuitions certainly seem to have been in accord with the notion in his choice of a suitable image.

The fourth feature to note is *the river*, which in the final scene flows into the unlimited ocean. Beginning as a modest stream, it becomes a beguiling, but deceptive, watercourse, then a raging torrent, before it meets with the calm expanse of the open sea. It represents, as we said, the flow of time; more specifically, it represents the flow of the Soul's time of earthly existence. That is to say, it is not simply "time" as a general reality, but time as the individual Soul experiences it. The river's rapids, for instance, represent the full variety of struggles, pain, distress, and fears encountered by every person. Such troubles are not the same for all, obviously, but no human being is without his or her fair share of troubles. They are, as we know, multiform. No two persons will face precisely the same evils in life, but each will face his or her own mixture of evils.

The fifth feature is *the landscape*. Like the river, the surrounding landscape changes from scene to scene. It is sufficient here to suggest only that the shifting landscape, drawn from Cole's close observation of nature both in America and abroad, is made to reflect both the stage in life the Soul has reached in each scene and his own inner condition. The ever-changing landscape, like the river, reveals the ever-changing nature of human development and experience. It indicates the impermanence of all things, including oneself.

The sixth and final feature to note, which also changes from scene to scene, is *the vantage point of the viewer*. Where does the viewer stand in relation to the scene he or she is viewing? Each of the paintings puts us in a new position regarding the boat, and we observe the Soul's journey from different angles. About the shifting of vantage points from painting to painting, Cole gave the practical explanation that he was expressing "a poetic thought," but doing so "picturesquely," by which he meant, as he went on to say, that if he "should be constrained to have the same view of the boat and figure or figures — nearly the same through the several parts of the work: this would be monotonous, and would strike the beholder as having arisen either from incompetency to execute, or from poverty of invention, and that pleasure which arises from novelty would entirely be lost."[11] Over and above the merely practical rationale of a craftsman, however, the different vantage points are important in that they serve to reveal to us something of the "inner" dimension of the Soul himself — how he is moved or resigned to what he is experiencing in each scene, how he is led or misled, how he is affected by his struggles, and his final composure at the time of death.

In the first painting, the boat with the infant Soul, manned by the Angel, comes *toward us* from the shadows of the dark cave. This is the image of emergence into earthly existence. The river is narrow, the banks are lush with vegetation, and the child's range of view is limited.

With the second scene, our vantage point shifts to somewhat *behind* the boat. Along with the youth, who has taken the tiller and is taking leave of the Angel, we look off into the distance toward a magnificent dream-future in the form of an Oz-like city. The painting affords us a vast — but deceptive — view of what the Soul confidently expects to be his destiny.

The third scene puts us once more in the position of having the boat moving *alongside* and slightly *toward us*. We are, as it were, on the bank watching the craft tossed and battered in the storm and by the rapids. There is no looking ahead into a wonderful, bright future now. Everything here is uncertain, threatening, in turmoil. It's a matter of survival we witness in this scene, and there is no sign of hope in front of the voyager. He prays in an agony that perhaps reminds the viewer of depictions of Christ in the Garden of Gethsemane. The hope we were allowed to glimpse in the second scene lies far behind the Soul now. However, there remains for him an unseen hope. We see it from

11 Noble, *Life and Works*, 211.

our vantage point outside the frame, but he cannot from within it. Above and behind him, above the looming crags and glowering clouds, but still guiding him with a ray of light, is the Angel. In some depictions of Christ's agony in the Garden, an angel is seen comforting him; in this scene, the Soul has no such consolation. He voyages "by faith, not by sight."

With the last scene, we are again looking at the aged Soul, this time from *off to his left* and somewhat *from behind*. The Angel—now fully visible to him—points him upward, through the parting storm clouds, to the heavenly light and other descending angels. His damaged boat lies becalmed on the surface of the infinite sea, the Soul having "ceased from all his labors." From our vantage point, we can look with him toward the promise that death affords.

In each of the paintings, then, the vantage point is important and skillfully conceived by Cole. Our viewpoint is either constrained or expanded as the scene requires. In each instance, we are joined sympathetically with the Soul in the vessel. It may be the most subtle of the six features, but the changing vantage points of the viewer are vital to the overall power of the series, and the artist pulls it off masterfully every time.

The cumulative effect of all six features, then, is a universal truth rendered in four arresting images. The series' meaning is recognizable to us, even if we're not immediately aware of how all the aspects and details are working on our minds. It might be tempting to say that the work depicts a "hero's journey," but that would be somewhat misleading, given popular ideas of what constitutes heroism. As touched on above, there is little in any of the scenes that can really be called "heroic" in the familiar sense of the term. The series is not a depiction of a conqueror, knight, or warrior, even though the youth in the second scene of the series is said to desire foolishly "a conqueror's crown"—a desire, in fact, that spells trouble for him later.[12] There is nothing like mythical or comic-book

12 Tymn, *Thomas Cole's Poetry*, 152. We might gain some insight into how Cole regarded a heroism that vaunted itself too highly, if we consider a sort of diptych that he worked on in 1837. The element of heroic tragedy was, of course, something of a Romantic trope. Still, it is suggestive when compared with the shifting of fortunes depicted in both of his most famous series of paintings (*The Course of Empire* and *Voyage*). In a letter, he described his conjoined Medieval scenes as follows:

"In the first picture, Morning, which I call The Departure, a dark and lofty castle stands on an eminence, embosomed in woods. The distance beyond is composed of cloud-capt mountains and cultivated lands, sloping down to the sea. In the foreground is a sculptured Madonna, by which passes a road, winding beneath ancient trees, and, crossing a stream by a Gothic bridge, conducting to the gate of the castle. From this gate has issued a troop of knights and soldiers in glittering armour: they are dashing down across the bridge and beneath the lofty trees, in the

superheroism in view, even if there appears to be an epic quality in all the scenes. This is not to deny that there is an evident element of courage on the part of the Soul, particularly apparent in the second and third scenes. But both scenes also depict naivete, disillusionment, miscalculation, downright terror, agonized supplication, and finally resignation to destiny. The triumph of the Soul in the final scene is that of one having *survived* the vicissitudes of earthly life, not having proved victorious by means of his own strength and cunning. The old Soul is "saved" at the end, rescued, and welcomed into eternity—his true home, one feels—by the familiar Angel. The glory at his end comes down to meet him; he has no glorious accomplishment of his own to carry upward. In the Christian faith that Cole espoused, salvation is a matter of grace (i.e., a gift, something unearned), and thus not one's own personal achievement.

Along with a notable absence of heroism, we should also acknowledge the melancholy atmosphere that pervades the scenes. This is by no accident, but by intent. We can "feel" it, perhaps only semiconsciously at first, in his choices, scene by scene, of chiaroscuro. Even in the second of the series, in which the youthful Soul looks ahead to a resplendent vision of the future, we can perceive an element of grim foreboding; we can see from our outside viewer's vantage point (although the youth within the painting obviously cannot "see" it from his) that the luminous vision in the sky is a deceiving illusion, and that turbulent waters instead are what actually await him beyond the diverting bend in the river ahead. What is straightforwardly acknowledged in these paintings is that sorrow attends human existence. It is seen to be an inescapable part of life from the very outset of the series, especially since we know in advance the destination toward which the river ultimately leads. Because of this foresight, the apparently joyful first scene of the infant Soul emerging into the world has already a pall over it. And we might ask, do the child's outstretched arms not only signify joy and surprise at the fresh vision before him, but also—by

---

foreground; and the principal figure, who may be the Lord of the Castle, reins in his charger, and turns a look of pride and exultation at the castle of his fathers and his gallant retinue. He waves his sword, as though saluting some fair lady, who from battlement or window watches her lord's departure to the wars. The time is supposed to be early summer.

"The second picture—The Return—is in early autumn. The spectator has his back to the castle. The sun is low: its yellow beams gild the pinnacles of an abbey, standing in a shadowy wood. The Madonna stands a short distance from the foreground, and identifies the scene. Near it, moving towards the castle, is a mournful procession; the lord is borne on a litter, dead or dying—his charger led behind—a single knight, and one or two attendants—all that war has spared of that once goodly company" (Noble, *Life and Works*, 182).

their cruciform position—hint at something more doleful to come, as in William Blake's "The Christ Child Asleep on a Cross," painted forty years earlier?

In this tendency to the melancholic, we recognize Cole as an exemplar of the Romantic mind. Romanticism was—to paint the age with a broad brush—a reaction to the Enlightenment's confident adulation of rationality. In contrast to the Romantic age, the Enlightenment idealized a cool and dispassionate temperament (an optimistic ideal betrayed only by that age's actual history). Romanticism, on the other hand, embraced subjective experience and the full range of human emotion. So it was that the melancholy atmosphere of Cole's four scenes (and most, if not all, of his oeuvre) was not perceived in his own day as just dreary or depressing, but as integral to *feeling* the truth of life realistically. Cole himself wrote, "I often think that the dark view of things is perhaps the true one." He didn't regard this as the only view, but as part and parcel of the full picture of reality (there must be *yin* as well as *yang*). As he continued: "If such a [dark] view were always presented, I doubt whether we could long survive. But Heaven has granted us a sunshine of the heart, that warms these barren cold realities of existence, and dazzles and deceives, perhaps, that we may live."[13] In his monumental study of the brain and how its two hemispheres, rightly understood, have had their impact on the history of the Western world, Iain McGilchrist notes that there is, in fact, a link between a sense of sadness and one's also having a grasp on reality: "If there is a tendency for the right hemisphere [of the brain] to be more sorrowful and prone to depression, this can . . . be seen as related . . . to being more in touch with what's going on . . ."[14]

Cole's four scenes, then, weren't an exercise in sheer fantasy. They allegorized what was felt to be real about human life, and allegory is never sheer fantasy. By invoking nature at its most sublime (expansive, uncontrollable, wild, overwhelming, even aesthetically unlovely) to achieve this end, the series taken as a whole was regarded as authentically *beautiful*.[15] It is important to note that "beauty" was not a weak category for the Romantics; the word wasn't a synonym for "lovely" or "pretty." On the contrary, for something to be "beautiful"

13 Noble, *Life and Works*, 164.

14 Iain McGilchrist, *The Master and His Emissary: The Divided Brain and the Making of the Western World* (New Haven and London: Yale University Press, 2009), 85.

15 Although, as we will see in our discussion of the third scene in Chapter V below, Cole would almost certainly not have called the "deformed nature" we see detailed in that particular scene "beautiful."

it had to be, by definition, seen as true, real, genuine; not shallow, superficial, trivial. Full-orbed beauty, therefore, includes melancholy because the appropriate, mature, and realistic emotional response to impermanence is precisely to experience it as the condition of ceaseless loss. In an age when people tended to be much more directly exposed to the presence of death and even decay, sadness was embraced as an unavoidable aspect of life's experience. It wasn't to be set aside or hidden away as something not to be endured. They recognized, as we tend not to, that loss awakens *longing* within us, both for what has passed and also for what awaits us beyond this life and our immediate senses. Longing and melancholy are intimately joined, then, and their joining is what creates the *beauty* we find expressed in art and poetry. When embraced and not shunned, it deepens our appreciation of life for all that it is, in all the fluctuation of its joys and sorrows. Sadness, as Edgar Allan Poe — Cole's contemporary — wrote with true insight, "is inseparably connected with all the higher manifestations of true Beauty."[16] He even described this profound, one could say mystical, variety of sadness as "pleasurable," though certainly not in the vapid sense of what we mean by "pleasure" today. It is "pleasurable" to the extent that it includes a longing for the ineffable. It is empathetic and spiritual in its intensity. Cole infused his pictorial allegory with this atmosphere of "pleasurable sadness," with the result that, once again, the series rings true.

*

With these few particulars in view, then, I turn to what one can expect from the remainder of this book. The chapter that follows is a cursory look at Thomas Cole, with special attention paid to his aesthetic and contemplative nature. He regarded himself as a poet as well as an artist, and although his poetry isn't esteemed highly or even remembered today except by very few, it isn't bad poetry. As we will see, his art and his poems together reveal a man of sensitivity, a keenly observant eye especially for the natural world, and an active and introspective mind. This will prepare us to see in the subsequent chapters how the paintings of *The Voyage of Life* are supplemented and interpreted by the long poem he wrote on the theme.

Following the chapter on Cole, then, I offer four essays, each of which deals with the four scenes in turn. These aren't intended as objective art criticism (if such a thing is possible) or art history, but only as individual reflections on

16 Edgar Allan Poe, "The Poetic Principle" in *The Complete Tales and Poems of Edgar Allan Poe* (London: Penguin Books, 1982).

the scenes. As is probably clear by now, I see them as dealing with perennial matters, first things that are true in every age, universal, essentially human. So, I look at these scenes subjectively, not attempting or, rather, pretending to "stand over" them, as if my critical eye is anything to brag about, but allowing them to inform my thoughts and feelings, recording how they have affected me. I hope to encourage readers to do the same for themselves, to look at Cole's art and allow it to "speak" to the soul. His is indeed, like all great art, made to feed the soul. We should approach it receptively, not as reviewers but as prepared for an interior encounter. We have far too many critics and too much criticism in our day (just look at the appalling critter we misname "social" media); what we need to relearn is the silent gaze, how to observe in stillness, the ability to allow something to impress itself upon us. That's where real philosophy happens—philosophy meaning literally a "love of wisdom." We obtain wisdom more through our quietness and introspection than by the words we hear. Words assist and guide, like fingers pointing at the moon, but it is whatever they point to that should ultimately get our attention.

In the following chapters I do offer words, a lot of them. I hope none of them is excessive. And I hope above all that this short book will be an invitation to look more closely at *The Voyage of Life* and Cole's works in general.

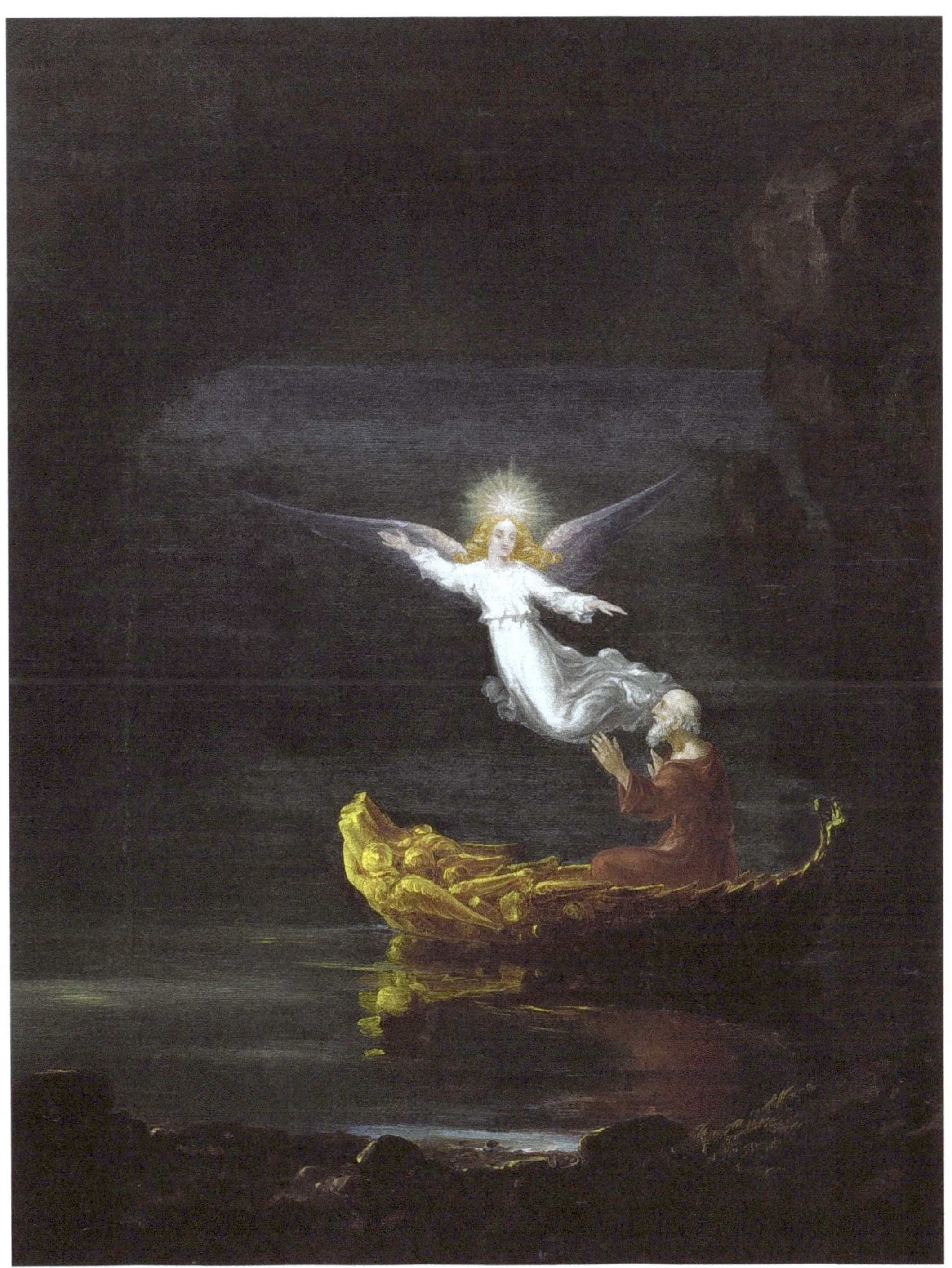

"OLD AGE," DETAIL

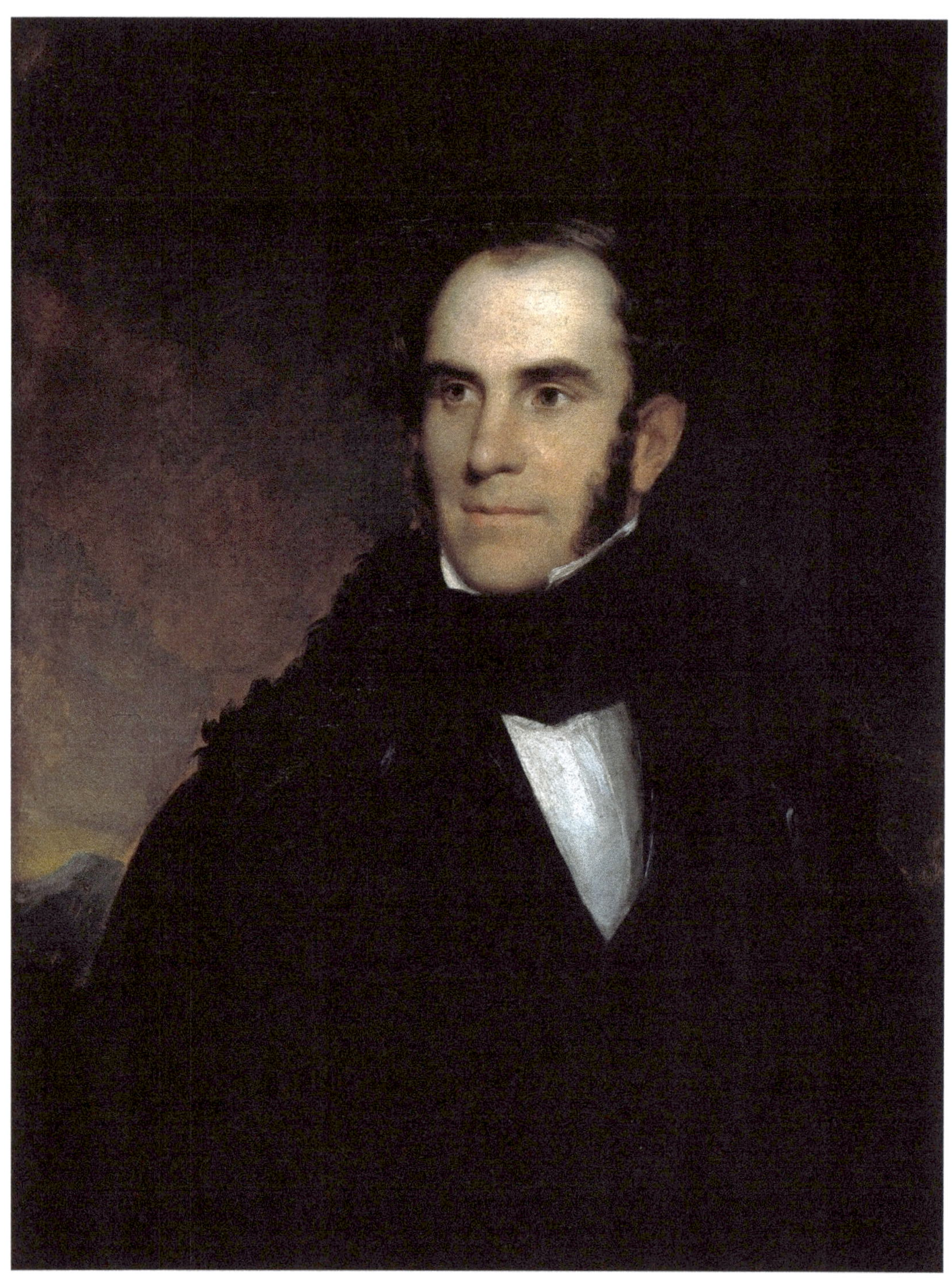

ASHER B. DURAND, "PORTRAIT OF THOMAS COLE" (1837)

II. Cole

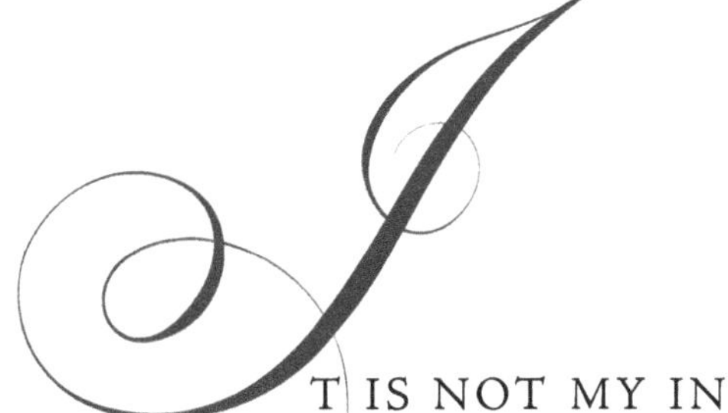

IT IS NOT MY INTENTION in this chapter to provide a detailed biographical sketch of Thomas Cole. The most basic facts of his relatively short life are as follows: he was born in England on February 1, 1801, and he died of pleurisy at the age of 47, at the height of his powers and acclaim, in Catskill, New York, on February 11, 1848. He emigrated to America with his family in 1819, when he was eighteen. He married in 1836, and he and his wife, Maria, had five children together. As an artist, he was mostly self-taught, learning from books and his study of other artists' work. As Cole became more and more revered for his landscape and allegorical paintings, he exercised an influence on other artists (for example, Frederic Church and Asher B. Durand) who together are remembered as constituting the Hudson River School of American art—a "school" of loosely connected 19th-century painters whose work was similar in subject matter and style, though they were not a "brotherhood" such as the Pre-Raphaelites in England were. Cole travelled overseas twice in his life, to Britain and the continent, becoming acquainted with some of the prominent British and European artists of the day. Mainly, though, he is justly noted for his renderings of the untamed American landscape, especially the mountainous regions of the Alleghenies. Those are the chief external facts of his biography, which can be supplemented with encyclopedia entries or by reading Noble's biography.

What I wish above all to do in this chapter, however, is focus on one key aspect—indeed, *the* key aspect—of Cole's character, which in turn made Cole what he was artistically. It is no criticism of the man to say that his outward day to day existence was not often eventful or dramatic. It doesn't make for exciting reading, but no one's recorded life need be that. It was in his inward life that all his vitality and warmth were to be found. That's where the action was, where the fire blazed. So it is that I intend to consider those interior qualities that gave birth to his art. To look as closely as we can at these elements of his character, to the extent that it's possible with anyone so far removed from us in time, will help us to see more in *The Voyage of Life* than might be the case otherwise.

Cole's biographer, Louis Legrand Noble, draws attention on more than one occasion to his subject's love of solitude and contemplation. Noble was a clergyman in the Episcopal Church, as well as Cole's close friend, a fellow poet, and a dabbler in "natural philosophy" (he was, it seems, impressively knowledgeable in Native American lore and language as well), so perhaps it should come as no surprise that he would highlight Cole's spiritual nature in his biography. *The Voyage of Life*, like most of Cole's works, reflects a temperament comfortable in its own company ("I am most happy when I can escape most from the world [of human traffic]"),[1] given to solitary reflection, and that looks upon the natural world with a keen eye, wonder, and awe. Noble informs us that Cole showed these tendencies from an early age. His family had come to America from Lancashire, England in 1819, when Thomas was eighteen. In that period of America's history, the wilderness was both everywhere to be experienced and—as Thomas was to lament throughout his life—destroyed by the encroachments of civilization (the latter constitutes one of the most salient themes of his series of paintings, *The Course of Empire*). Cole sought to experience America's natural wildness, then, at a time when it was undergoing domestication, exploitation, and ruin at the hands of industrialists and developers. In his sharp dislike for this state of affairs, he reminds us of Thoreau, and in fact there is some notable philosophical and spiritual commonality between Cole and Thoreau (and also Emerson).

Cole was not baptized into the church until 1842 when, at the age of 41, Noble himself baptized him. In his biography of Cole, though, Noble has no hesitation affirming that the former had always been a man of spiritual depth and a natural contemplative. By "contemplation" I mean precisely "religious" or "spiritual musing"—the word originally meant to be "with" or "within" an area or place (*templum*, temple) where augury or divination was practiced. To "contemplate" means to "look attentively" or "to behold" (in the case of divination, it meant to "look closely" or to "read" the signs), but the word has acquired

---

1 Noble, *Life and Works*, 151.

over centuries of Western spirituality a quite different reference, that of solitary interior practice — silent meditation, in particular. This should not be confused with a state of mere passivity; on the contrary, it requires a mind that is alert and aware. It is a heightened mental state, one of wakefulness, not drowsiness or daydreaming. One detects almost a note of mysticism in Noble's description of Cole's attention to unspoiled nature — "a passion for nature was his ruling passion . . . The tones and expressions of the outer world found answering tones and expressions in his soul. *He was beginning to behold in that something of himself, and to see in himself something of that.*" That description is almost a meditation in itself.[2]

Cole wrote in his personal journal that "nature has secrets known only to the initiated. To him she speaks in the most eloquent language."[3] If we were to ask, then, where Cole encountered the transcendent, beginning at an early age, the answer is clearly in the reciprocity between the nature he observed and the interiority he cultivated. The *templum* in which he contemplated was both within himself and within the natural world he encountered. He had an inner awareness of the mystical connection between himself and all things. Noble makes another remarkable observation about Cole's interiority: "Cole clearly saw, and heartily rejoiced in the great and all-pervading principle of the universe, *unity arising out of infinity*. As in the humblest object, a pebble or a fungus, there is a hint, an expression of the infinite, so in the innumerable assemblage of all things there is a language eloquently expressive of unity. Infinitude in each; a harmonious union, a oneness out of all. To realize this was Cole's, at an early period."[4]

There was a stage in the development of Cole's art that Noble describes as a sudden revelation that came to him. He had been dissatisfied with his early efforts. They struck him as mere imitation, stiff and lifeless, lacking vitality and feeling. Then, all at once, it dawned on him how he might rectify that deficiency and transform his art into animated (in the sense of possessing "soul"), vibrant renderings of his subject matter. It would require a meticulous, focused, methodical attention to what he observed — a sort of open-eyed, almost

2 Ibid., 11. Emphasis added. This sentence of Noble's puts me in mind of that passage in Martin Buber's *I and Thou*, in which Buber speaks of contemplating a tree: "I contemplate a tree . . . But it can also happen, if will and grace are joined, that as I contemplate the tree I am drawn into a relation, and the tree ceases to be an It . . ." Martin Buber, *I and Thou*, trans. and annot. by Walter Kaufman (New York: Simon and Schuster, 1996), 57–58.

3 Noble, *Life and Works*, 41.

4 Ibid., 56. Emphasis in the original.

Zenlike gaze, scrutinizing every detail in an ascending order. "Hitherto," Noble explains, "he had been trying mainly to make up nature from his own mind, instead of making up his mind from nature. This now flashed upon him as a radical mistake." The result of this sudden realization on Cole's part was that he adopted an entirely new practice:

> At its first and last light, many a spring, summer, and autumnal day found him on the wild banks of the Monongahela [River], carefully drawing, from the crinkled root that lost itself in the mould to "the one red leaf... on the topmost twig that looks up at the sky"—to the mountain-line on the skirts of the sky—to the clouds far up in the sky, and the blue sky far away from the clouds.[5]

Note the "ladder of ascent" here, how Cole's eye is said to have roved up and up, step by step, from the minutiae of the vegetal to the infinity beyond the horizon. This rigorous practice of an ascending observation from the roots of trees to the vastness of the sky, taking in everything in between, becomes evident to us when we examine a painting of Cole's in the knowledge that this was his procedure. Cole directs our gaze ever beyond and deeper. He became a master of depicting "depth," so important to landscape painters in the West from the Renaissance onward.

Some pages further on, Noble gives us yet another stirring glimpse of Cole's practice of *looking* in wonder at scenery, even at landscapes he had seen many times before, in search of what Noble calls, without defining it, "spirit":

> He went, at the hundredth time, as one going for the first time—not in words, not in outward excitement, but in all gentleness and quietness, and in spirit, for he went to seek spirit: and when he found it under the shuck and crust of things, shuck and crust were all beating and throbbing with life; they were living creatures, ever beautiful, ever new: and so the last time of looking was as the first, and nature grew to him youthful instead of older, and covered tokens of heaven and immortality in its mouldering trunks, as ashes cover the living coals.[6]

---

5 Ibid., 23–24. See also: McGilchrist, *The Master and His Emissary*, 247: "Even to attend to anything so closely that one can capture its essence is not to copy slavishly. To Ruskin it was one of the hardest, as well as one of the greatest human achievements, truly to see, so as to copy and capture the life of, a single leaf—something the greatest artists had managed only once or twice in a life time: 'If you can paint *one* leaf, you can paint the world.' Imitating nature may be like imitating another person's style; one enters into the life. Equally that life enters into the imitator."

6 Noble, *Life and Works*, 54.

This is a lovely passage, evocative in its depiction of what Cole saw in nature; it is likewise a very accurate description of what he put on canvas.

When we look at one of Cole's renderings of natural grandeur, we are struck by two things: first, its attention to the actual details of what he saw, and second, that it is simultaneously a transfigured landscape. Something of the numinous shines through it—his style isn't simply realistic. Cole, like other Romantic painters, gives us nature as a sacrament, an "outward and visible sign of an inward and spiritual grace." Cole would have agreed with the sentiment accredited to Meister Eckhart, that every natural *thing* is a word of God—everything, that is, has something innate to it, that lies also beyond it, which that thing manifests. "The world is charged with the grandeur of God. / It will flame out, like shining from shook foil."[7] Evelyn Underhill wrote:

> In those hours [when the sense of beauty is felt], the world has seemed charged with a new vitality; with a splendour which does not belong to it but is poured through it, as light through a coloured window, grace through a sacrament, from that Perfect Beauty which "shines in company with the celestial forms" beyond the pale of appearance.[8]

As florid as Underhill's description might seem to us today (she wrote it in 1911), it nevertheless accords with a Romantic sensibility that Cole shared. What he was after was the truth that lay behind what he was portraying. If all things "live, move, and have their being" in God,[9] as Cole believed, then we could say that Cole endeavored to make his portrayals of the sublime and beautiful reflective of that belief.

We see this even in the relative proportions of human figures and the rest of the natural world in his depictions (as we also do in other Romantic artists, for example, the German Caspar David Friedrich). In such pieces as *Falls of the Kaaterskill* (1826) and *Scene from "The Last of the Mohicans," Cora Kneeling at the Feet of Tamenund* (1827), the human figures are dwarfed by their surroundings—great mountains, glowering skies, storm-blasted landscapes, forbidding rock formations, yawning crevasses, cascading sheets of water, twisted trunks of trees. Nature is big, man is small. Like Chinese, Korean, and Japanese art, Cole depicts human figures in the context of nature as only a small part of it, and not the most significant part. Unlike Chinese, Korean, and Japanese art, his

---

7 Gerard Manley Hopkins, "God's Grandeur."

8 Evelyn Underhill, *Mysticism: A Study in the Nature and Development of Man's Spiritual Consciousness* (New York: Meridian Books, 1956), 22.

9 Acts 17:28.

scenes do not "emerge" out of emptiness or mist but are relatively "hard" and full of colorful detail. The nature he depicts isn't evanescent (although, in fact, he dreaded the actual loss of the wilderness he loved) but appears everlasting and everlastingly daunting in relation to man. However, the *proportionality*—which is not atypical of landscape art in the West or of the Hudson River School in particular—nonetheless says to us philosophically what Eastern art tends to say, as well: human beings stand small in relation to the much greater reality of earthly nature. We are just passing through this world (like the voyaging Soul in *The Voyage of Life*); we don't own nature, despite our grossly oversized presumption. It's bigger and more resilient and more enduring than we are. Human beings are comparative specks. It will abide in one form or another, regardless of what happens to us.

Returning to the subject of Cole as contemplative, when we understand that that trait was basic to his disposition, then—as we shall see—everything else about *The Voyage of Life* falls into place. First and foremost, the entire series should be viewed as a spiritual or mystical interpretation of human life. He was comfortable with metaphor and allegory—a feature of art that was ironized and eroded later on by the Modernists. What Robert Hughes failed to understand, as we saw in the last chapter, and what other critics of Cole's allegorical works have sometimes also failed to see, is that Cole wasn't a pedant. His allegories don't "lecture" to us, even at their most didactic. He's not a mere moralist, and so Hughes's brusque estimation of *The Voyage of Life* as so much "Victorian kitsch"—a phrase that suggests moralism in the worst sense—rings false, or at least it does to my ears.

Rather, Cole shows us what he has *seen*—he's a "seer," and he gives us "visions" in paint. He wasn't a visionary in the sense that, say, William Blake was. He certainly never saw himself as some sort of prophet, conversing familiarly with Old Testament figures and angels. He was, however, gifted with imagination—which is not the same thing as a mere fantasist—and by that power a painter of vivid allegory. Allegory isn't simply symbolism, although allegory involves the use of symbols. Rather, it is like a parabolic story. It tells a story that is more than just a story. It doesn't *require* explanation, even if an explanation is subsequently provided (Cole's poem on the series, as we will see, in fact offers one, and we will rely on it throughout this book—but even without his poem, the paintings could speak for themselves). Allegory *shows* us and allows us to make the necessary connections. Cole's allegorical works are visionary, hence metaphorical, hence (in the best sense of the term) "mystical."

Cole, though not a "practicing mystic" himself, undeniably had the Romantic's mystical tendency. This is clearly seen in the lengthy poem, based on the four scenes, that Cole composed in 1844, four years after the series' completion. He wrote it as consolation for the death of a friend and colleague, reminding us just how substantially death figures in the series' meaning. All the scenes lead up to death and what follows it—there is a *memento mori* aspect of the series that can't be ignored. Cole's poem begins in a wood, reminiscent of the opening cantos of Dante's *Inferno*:

> Forth through the ancient shadowy woods as one
> Who hath no being but his thought I wended
> Instinctively. The deep and solemn tone,
> The holy gloom harmoniously blended
> With musings grave and fond of Life and Death
> And immortality; which waits our parting breath.

As the four scenes unfold before him as visions, Cole has a dialogue with his own soul, which in turn serves as a guide and narrator elucidating the scenes to him (in this, too, we are reminded of Dante's three successive guides, Virgil, Beatrice, and St. Bernard of Clairvaux, who lead the Florentine through Hell, Purgatory, and Heaven). But it is Cole's own soul that is personified in the role of guide. In other words, it becomes an "other" in relation to him. If, as I suggested in the previous chapter, the Angel and the Soul are to be regarded together as "higher" and "lower" aspects of a single person, then the same might be said of the role played by Cole's soul in the poem. It is, in a sense, Cole's "Angel," the inner "higher" voice or intuition which he must trust and heed. So, regarding the very first scene, in which the new-born Soul emerges from the cave and the Angel is depicted guiding the vessel, Cole writes:

> "What meaneth this," with earnest voice I cried,
> "The landscape bright, the river's flow serene,
> And those two Voyagers—"[10] My soul replied:
> "Life hath her pictures of each varied scene
> The mortal pilgrim sees, wrought on the heart
> In colors clear and strong that never can depart..."[11]

We will come back to this poem often in the pages ahead, but for now we want only to point out that it confirms that Cole's own understanding of

---

10 The "two Voyagers" are, of course, the Soul as an infant and the Angel.

11 Tymn, *Thomas Cole's Poetry*, 145–46.

his work was spiritual in nature. The poem indicates, too, that this series was an especially significant work for him, one that emerged from his reflections on life and death (he would himself be dead less than four years after the writing of the poem). It constitutes his own personal *Divine Comedy*.

Unlike Dante's great poem, however, it isn't "vertical," but "horizontal" in conception. Dante first *descends* into the earth and then *ascends* steeply, via the mount of Purgatory in the Antipodes, from the depths to the heights. In contrast, Cole's voyager is *borne along* on the current of time from the darkness of a cave entrance to the open sea, from whence he will be gathered up to heaven. Dante's vision is primarily spatial; Cole's is primarily temporal. Cole's spiritual vision is earthbound, surrounded in every scene by the natural world; his voyager is, as it were, passing through this sphere. We can perhaps infer that this tells us something significant about the character of Cole's spirituality: it begins in this world, amid earthly nature, and stays within its terrestrial context right through to the end. Cole's axiom, as Noble called it, had in fact been "to walk with nature as a poet is the necessary condition of a perfect artist."[12] The Soul in *The Voyage of Life* isn't walking, but he continues "with nature" all through his river journey.

Cole was not only alert to the details and wonders of nature but possessed and cultivated a profound empathy with it. "Feeling" was important to him; his art is imbued with it. It went hand in hand with his awareness of the connection that exists between all living things. There is something of the Taoist's sensitivity to nature and the Buddhist's sensitivity to the world's sufferings to be found in Cole, as there is in Emerson and Thoreau. Regarding the latter, Noble tells us, "He could not himself bear to inflict, nor to see others inflict, pain upon the meanest animal; and hence he could never be taught to love the sports of the huntsman or the angler." This was not just squeamishness on his part, but something that went deeper in him, and—according to Noble—it was "religious" in nature:

> He had a profound sense of the antagonisms of life, and of the deep yearning of humanity for release and consolation under the spiritual blight that had fallen upon it, and of which innumerable things in the material world were mournfully typical. This lively consciousness of moral distinctions, the sensibility to suffering, this sense of the bitter contrasts of life, and of the sadness and sorrow which human

12 Noble, *Life and Works*, 39.

> life and nature both do really express—which sadness and sorrow are virtually a mute prayer to be set free, and comforted—these all were Cole's in an eminent degree. And so his was truly a religious temperament...[13]

This passage might remind us of the legend of the young Prince Siddhartha Gautama who, upon discovering the profound sorrows of the world, went on his ascetical quest and eventually became the Buddha. And Cole's empathy for nature extended even to the non-animal living world—we could say it extended to all "sentient beings" and beyond. One of his poems, written in 1834, decries the cutting down of a favorite tree: "O! ruthless was the deed / Destroying man! What demon urg'd the speed / Of thine unpitying axe? Didst thou not know / My heart was wounded by each savage blow?" This lamentation in turn leads him to reflect, Buddhist-like, on the universal verity of impermanence: "Vain is my plaint! All that I love must die... again shall spread o'er me / Never the gentle shade of my beloved tree—"[14] Noble tells us that this sensitivity to sorrow and suffering—his "religious temperament"—was a preparation for his late-in-life conversion to Christianity: "A temperament like his could only bloom and fructify in the full light and warmth of Christianity. Short of that, nothing would be able to satisfy his spiritual longings."[15] As we shall see as we delve into the four scenes of *The Voyage of Life*, and as we have seen implied already in Noble's descriptions of Cole, both men's Christianity appears to have been broadminded, saturated—healthily, I think—with the best religious currents of Romanticism, as was true both of the "broad church" and "high church" Anglicanism of their age.

That said, Noble considered *The Voyage of Life* a monumental but spiritually immature work. His judgment of it was that, while "it had the superior virtue of a Christian character," it was "the work of a man in the infancy of the divine life, with its dawning only upon him, its noon far before him, his views of the gospel partial and incomplete, and hence... incongruous and imperfect." To Cole, however, he notes that the work "was dear to him for the reason that it was a memorial of the time when his heart was moving into the blessed religion of Jesus Christ." "It would serve," Noble concludes, "to mark the childhood of his Christian character as later works would mark its manhood."[16]

---

13 Ibid., 58.
14 Tymn, *Thomas Cole's Poetry*, 67.
15 Noble, *Life and Works*, 58.
16 Ibid., 287.

I believe we can chalk up those sentiments of Noble's to his wishful thinking. He was, at the end of the day, a clergyman with certain doctrinal commitments (for example, as we will touch on in the next chapter, he would have been committed to the belief that all persons are conceived with original sin, and therefore aren't born innocent—a doctrine Cole did not accept; as Cole put it in his poem, "innocence enshrines the infant-heart"). Perhaps Noble had wished to see more explicit Christian symbolism, such as the cross, in Cole's art, and Cole indeed did propose—and started on—a series with overt Christian imagery (*The Cross and the World*). But, that unrealized series aside, there is no notable "maturing" of Cole's implicit spirituality in his later works, even in his more explicitly Christian work. There can be no doubt that he was actively and seriously practicing his faith in his last years. On the small writing table in his "painting-room" during his last days, Noble informs us, Cole had "a Bible filled with marks, the Book of Common Prayer, and Bishop Wilson's Sacra Privata."[17] But the fact that *The Voyage of Life* remained "dear to him" suggests that he regarded it as abidingly expressive of an important aspect of his spiritual vision. Additionally, the fact that he wrote his explanatory poem in 1844, two years after his baptism and less than four years before his death, tells us how important the work continued to be for him. His other poetry written during those years is also congruent with his earlier sentiments regarding nature, man, and God. So it is that, Noble's assessment notwithstanding, I tend to the opinion that *The Voyage of Life* gives us real insight not into an immature spiritual vision on the part of Cole, but into his mature one. It is the fruit of his contemplation, not acquired doctrine, born of prayer and experience, not of a theological system. It is both simple and profound simultaneously, as the best spirituality tends to be. It is allegorical and earthy both, not hung up in abstruse metaphysics but, as said before, intelligible to the common viewer.

Among Cole's last poems, there is one in particular that stands out, in my opinion, as a succinct articulation of his penetrating spiritual perception, and which in addition draws together some of the thematic threads we can see in *The Voyage of Life*. It is the poem of a contemplative, one who possesses genuine insight into the impermanent nature of this earthly life and with it a living hope for the next, who knows himself to be only "passing through," and whose wide-awake sadness over all that must pass and be abandoned is the

---

17 Ibid., 298.

antithesis of despair—it is, on the contrary, formative of a deep longing. With it, I end this chapter before moving on to explore our series of four paintings. Here, then, is Cole the contemplative:

> 'Tis all a dream: our joys, our fears
> Our hopes a dream—The spirit hath existence
> But now it sleeps, of its earthly sleep
> These are the feverish visions—The waking time
> Draws near, when all such ill-form'd phantasies
> Shall flee away like night-clouds from the sun—
> A morn shall dawn: a bright mid-day arrive
> Then the reality of being shall be known
> In the full glory of eternal life—[18]

18 Tymn, *Thomas Cole's Poetry*, 200.

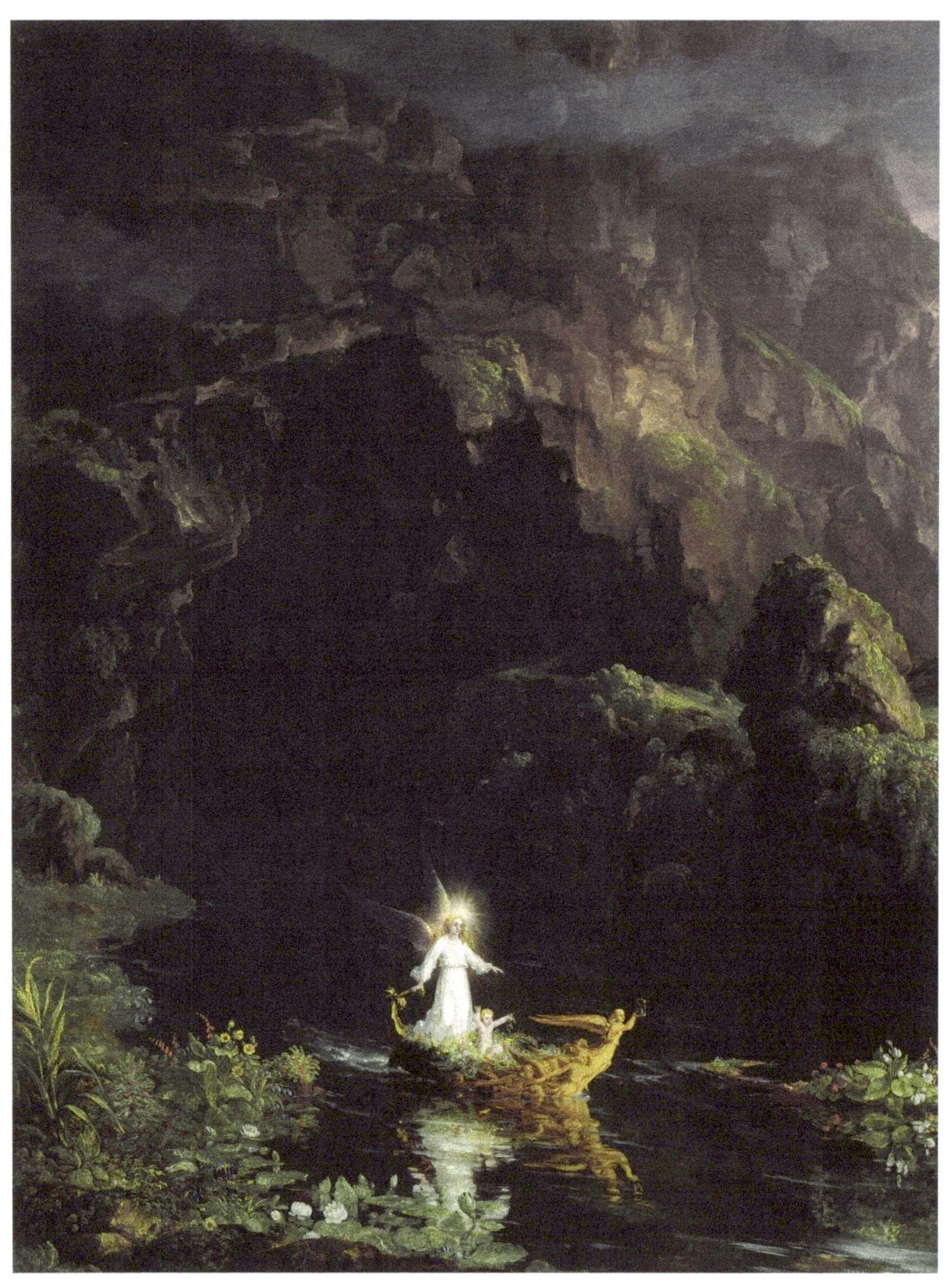

"CHILDHOOD," DETAIL

III. "Childhood"

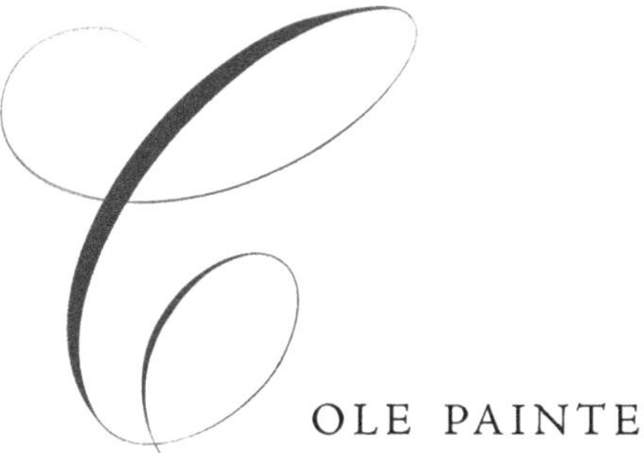

OLE PAINTED *The Expulsion from the Garden of Eden* in 1828.[1] It is a large painting, measuring 39.75 inches by 54.5 inches. Some elements of this earlier monumental scene are strikingly similar to features found in *The Voyage of Life*. Looking at it, we see that the Garden of Eden, to the viewer's right, is lush and sunlit. Mountains and a river or tarn can be seen in the background. Two swans swim at leisure in a smaller, calmer body of water nearer the foreground, and from the latter issues a modest waterfall. Here is nature shown as paradisial, beautiful, and inviting. In contrast, to the viewer's left, we see another kind of landscape entirely. It is the wilderness outside Eden, and it is dark, violent, windswept, blasted. A volcano is shown erupting in the distance.[2] Here depicted is nature at its most sublime, hideous, and frightening. Between the Garden and the wilderness, Cole has imagined for us a gigantic portal

---

1 Today it is displayed at the Museum of Fine Arts in Boston, Massachusetts.

2 Cole would have known something of the shocking force of volcanic eruptions. One of his poems, "Mt. Etna," was written in May of 1842, just after he had journeyed up that volcanic mountain ("But for yon filmy smoke, that from thy crest / Continual issues; there would be no sign / That from thy mighty breast bursts forth at times / The sulphurous storm—the avalanche of fire; / That midnight is made luminous and day / A ghastly twilight by thy lurid breath." Tymn, *Thomas Cole's Poetry*, 134–35).

We can have little doubt, as well, that he would have recalled the 1815 eruption of Mount Tambora and its cataclysmic effects, the deadliest and most powerful eruption in recorded history. At the time, he was fourteen and still living in England. In addition to 92,000 killed, the effects from the volcanic blast were felt worldwide. One such consequence was "the year without a summer" in 1816. Mary Shelley's *Frankenstein* was conceived at Lake Geneva, Switzerland, that same summer. The inclement weather that resulted from the eruption had kept her, her family members, and friends cooped up indoors. One of their pastimes during this time of inconvenience—now a matter of literary history—was to invent scary stories.

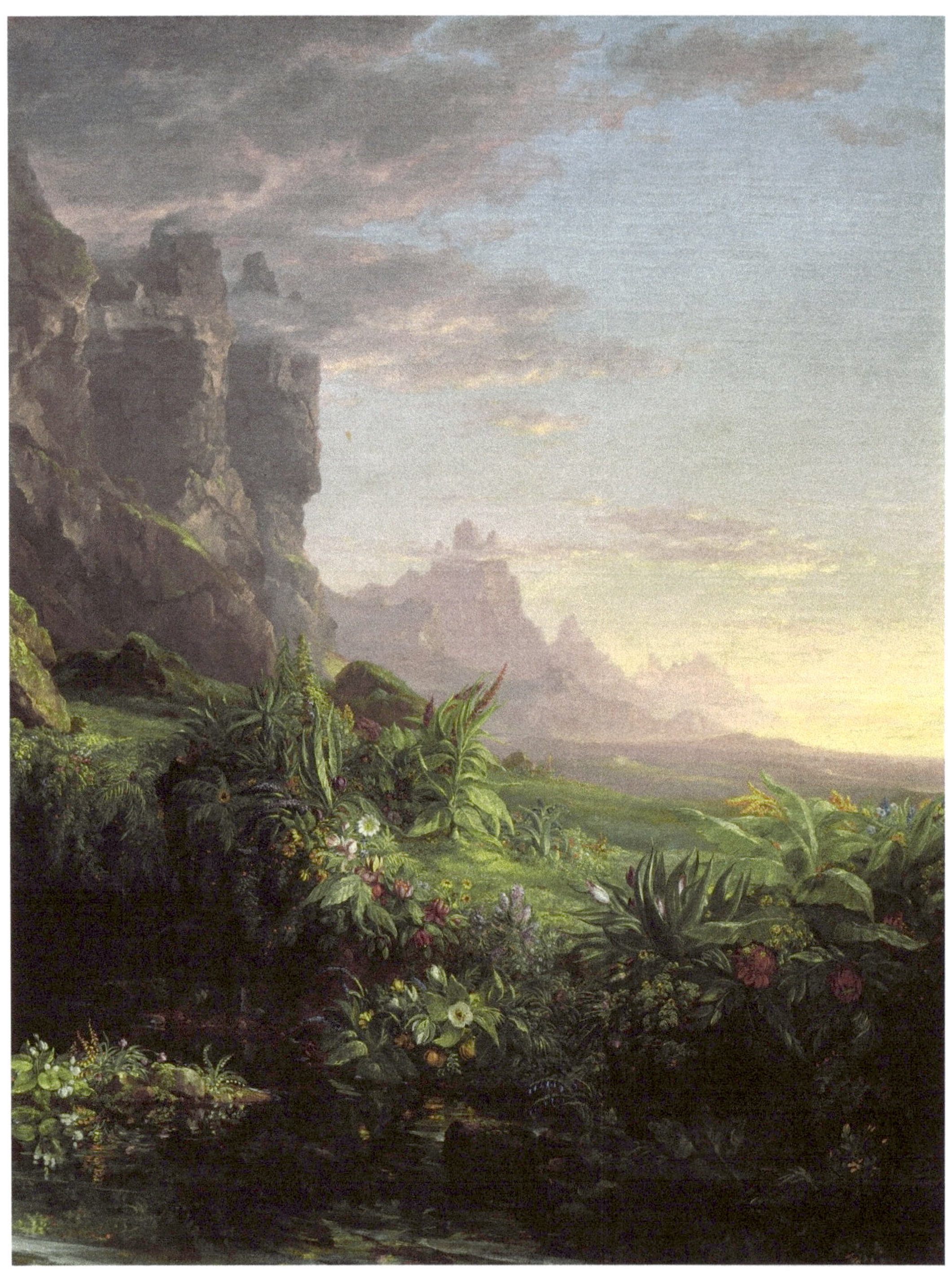

"CHILDHOOD," DETAIL

of stone. An immense bridge, also of rough-hewn stone, spans another, far fiercer cataract than the smaller waterfall mentioned above. The two tiny figures of Adam and Eve can barely be descried, dwarfed as they are by the terrifying landscape. They flee in evident dismay out of Eden and into the turbulence of the wilderness. Behind them, streaming from the portal, is the light of, presumably, the "cherubim" and the flaming sword mentioned at the conclusion of the third chapter of Genesis.

I bring up this earlier work of Cole's before examining the first scene of *The Voyage of Life* for two reasons. First and most obvious, as mentioned above, in it we find a number of similarities to elements found in the later series. The lushness of the Garden, with its greenery and flowers, swaying palms and tranquil waters, reminds us of features we see in the first and second scenes of *Voyage*. The wilderness outside Eden, with its glowering crags, stormy and clouded skies, its atmosphere of overwhelming menace, its horrible desolation, looks like a grander vision of the comparably horrible landscape through which the Soul travels in the third scene ("Manhood").

But the second reason for beginning with a glance back at this earlier work is that, despite these obvious surface similarities, there could seem to us, at a deeper level, to be some difference of theological-anthropological perspective between it and that of *Voyage*. At least, we might be tempted to assume so on first consideration (I admit that I did).

The reason for suspecting this is the case is understandable enough. *The Expulsion* presents us with a scene taken from the ancient story of "the fall of man (and woman)." As told in the Genesis narrative and embroidered by later traditions, it recounts how the first human pair was created pristine and unsullied, and how, through the machinations of the serpent (the devil), they disobeyed and were expelled from God's presence. Consequently, all the descendants of Adam and Eve — the entire human race, that is — are born in sin and bear the guilt of Adam and Eve's original rebellious act. In the West, this inclusion of the entire race in Adam and Eve's culpability (because, as ancient people saw it, we were all contained in "Adam's seed"), a culpability passed down from generation to generation, has been called "original sin."[3] Cole faithfully and elaborately illustrates the story's crucial event: the original pair are banished. Consequently, we were all banished with them. Adam and Eve's

---

3 In the East, the churches have held a markedly different view than that of the West. The term used is not "original sin," but "ancestral sin," and what is inherited is death and spiritual infirmity — but not guilt for the disobedience of Adam and Eve.

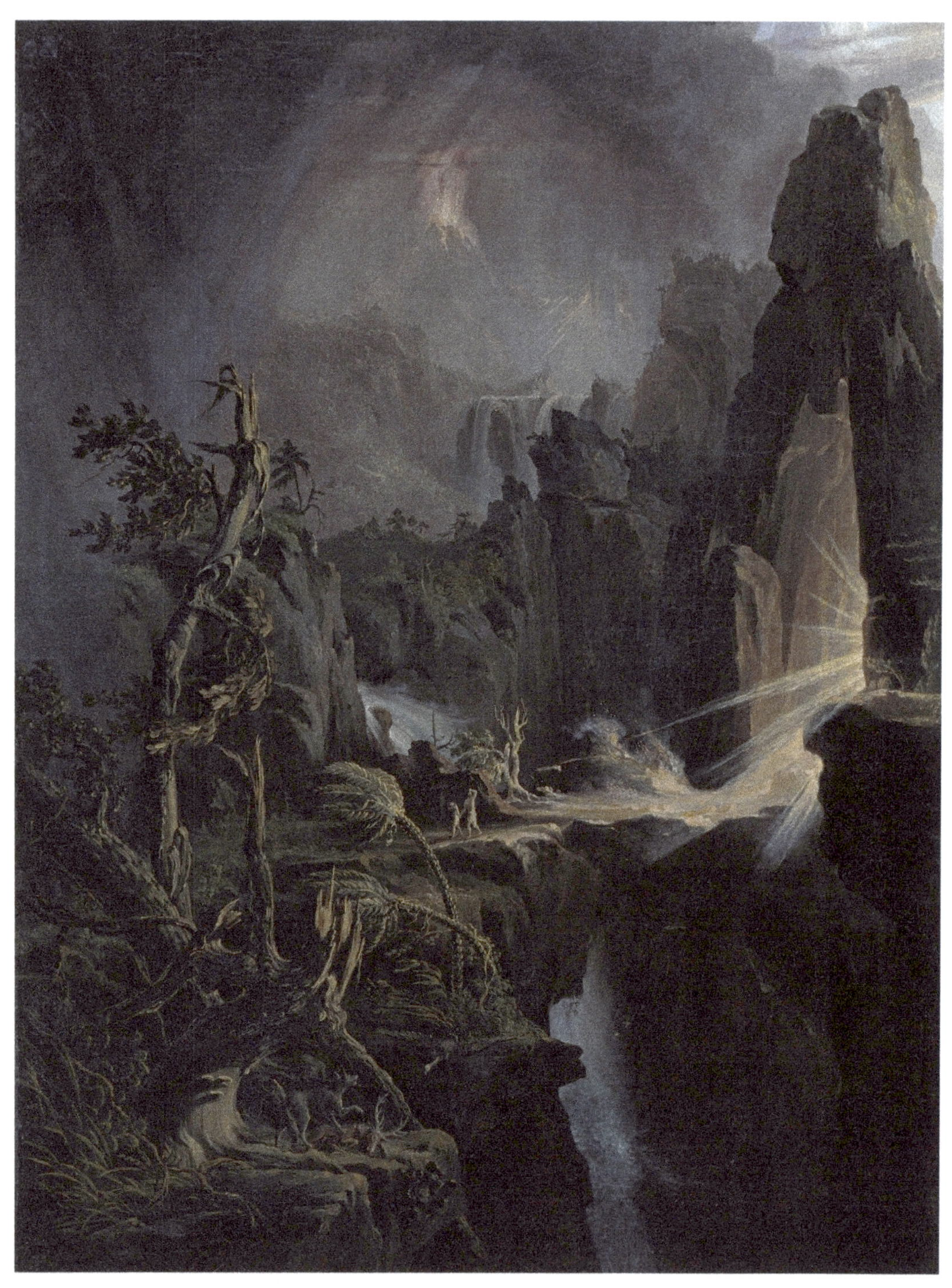

"THE EXPULSION FROM THE GARDEN OF EDEN"

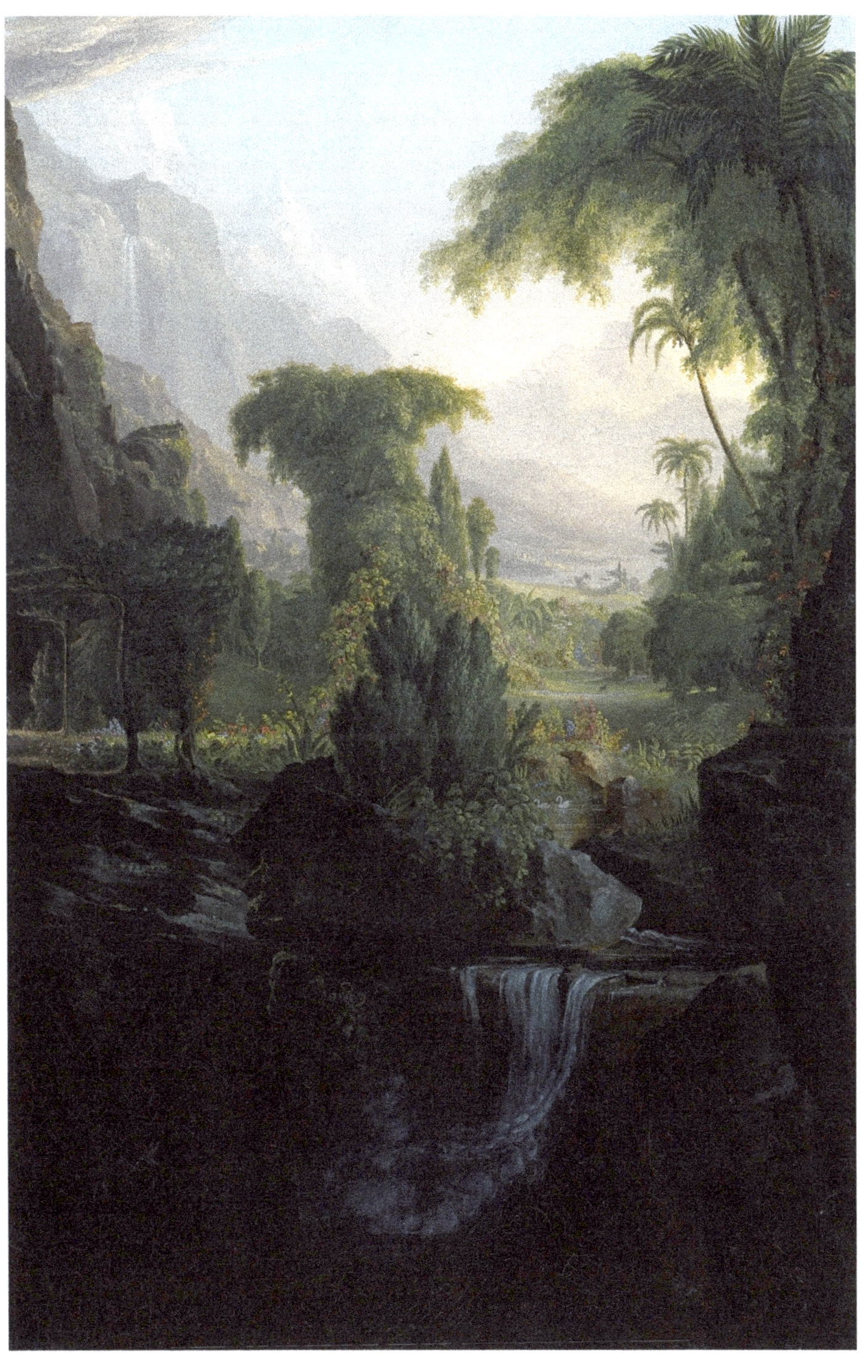

ejection from Eden and from unmediated communion with God is the plight we share, as well. Worse news still, we carry within ourselves our first parents' guilt from the moment of our conception. We are lost sinners before ever we can sin actively, born corrupted and condemned to hell from the start. We can only be freed from this condition by an act of God's sovereign grace. As I say, Cole depicts a scene from this old familiar story, and to the majority of the painting's viewers, the theological baggage would have been regarded simply as part and parcel of the tale.

But did Cole himself accept this accumulation of theological baggage? Did he regard every human being as conceived in sin and born guilty and condemned? It seems, in fact, that he did not. He viewed, as we will see, each person as born in innocence, and whatever "fall" each of us inevitably experiences in life is our individual reliving of the story in Genesis. Nothing in *The Expulsion* suggests that Cole believed he was painting a strictly historical scene. This is not to presume to speak on his behalf concerning what precisely he believed in the privacy of his own thoughts concerning the historiography of the Bible, but what is seen in his painting is clearly the juxtaposition of two fantastic landscapes, both highly metaphorical in their features. It appears to be as allegorical in intent as his other allegorical works. The power of *The Expulsion*, then, lies in its emblematic nature. What we should see in it is a theme he would later illustrate more fully—and maybe even more truly as regards his own belief—in *Voyage*: the loss of our original, ineffectual innocence and the providential soul-forming involvement we must undergo individually in the pains of this world in order that we might grow, through struggle and sorrow (not unmixed with joy and delight), into the attainment of higher things. Cole articulates this expressly in his explanatory poem for *Voyage*:

> "A higher destiny is thine," replied
> My soul "through trial, sorrow, darkness, pain
> The road to far sublimer joys does lead
> And lasting bliss by suffering we gain
> And by the gloomy vale through which we tread
> We reach the bliss that makes all earthly joy seem dead."[4]

What we ought to see, then, in Cole's terrifying vision of the wilderness, both in *The Expulsion* and later in the third scene of *Voyage*, is something akin

4 Tymn, *Thomas Cole's Poetry*, 148.

to Keats's "vale of Soul-Making" (Cole's "gloomy vale"[5]), rather than an image simply of punishment and banishment. Neither a curse nor a blessing, it is an allegory of life—the intermingling of opposites, beautiful and sublime, good and evil, joy and sorrow—understood as a "school" for the soul (to use Keats's language).[6] If we look at *The Expulsion* in these terms, then the differences between it and the allegory of *Voyage* are nugatory at best. It is *Voyage*, however, that gives us the much richer, broader picture of the concept that Cole wanted to illustrate in these works.

Cole's poem leaves us in little doubt that he believed firmly in "original innocence" as opposed to "original sin." In Part One, his guide—his soul—says as much regarding the infant in "the richly freighted bark":

> "Know! *innocence enshrines the infant-heart*
> Its tears are but as dew drops freshening joy;
> For *withering sin, as yet, can claim no part*
> Nor pale remorse bedim the beaming eye.
> Children are buds of Heaven *'tis earthly air*
> *That breeds the cankers, guilt and deadening despair*."[7]

The poem is abundantly clear on the point: the infant is innocent; sin claims no part of his emergent life, and only his existence in this "earthly air" (that is, this world of intermingled qualities) threatens to plant the seeds of future guilt in his heart. In the painting we see only innocence reflected in the features of the infant Soul, seated and draped as he is in flowers, his arms outstretched in wonder. Perhaps, as I mentioned in the first chapter, those outstretched arms portend a future "crucifixion." William Blake had painted his "Christ Child Asleep on a Cross" in 1799/80, and so the disturbing association of an infant and a cross wasn't without some artistic precedent, nor would it have been a notion foreign to Cole's overall theme. I am not wholly convinced that that was Cole's intention, but the idea is intriguing, nonetheless. At any rate, the

5 Cole uses the same image of a pilgrim passing through "the gloom of that dread valley [of this life]" in an earlier poem, "Life's Pilgrimage" (dated January 1, 1843, during the period he was working on the *Voyage* series of paintings). Ibid., 137–39.

6 "I will call the *world* a School instituted for the purpose of teaching little children to read—I will call the *human heart* the *horn Book* used in that School—and I will call the *Child able to read, the Soul* made from that *school* and its *hornbook*. Do you not see how necessary a World of Pains and troubles is to school an Intelligence and make it a soul? A Place where the heart must feel and suffer in a thousand diverse ways!" John Keats, "letter to his brother George, April 21, 1819" in *Selected Letters*, ed. John Barnard (London: Penguin Books, 2014).

7 Tymn, *Thomas Cole's Poetry*, 148. Emphasis added.

universal child he depicts is innocent. "The infant lives in the present," wrote Cole in a letter, describing the painting. "It neither looks back into the past, nor forward into the future. It enjoys the strange world into which it has come; but its views and capacities are limited to a very small circle."[8]

The Angel, with her starry brow, has the tiller and is the guiding intelligence that oversees the voyage at this stage: "One hand the Vessel's rudder graceful pressed, / The other stretched with benignant care / O'er the child."[9] The day is dawning, it's a glorious morning, a new beginning. This is seen in the colors Cole has chosen for the mountains, the sky, and the vanishing point to the viewer's right — mauves and rose, soft blues and yellow where the sun rises. These are all suggestive of newness, freshness, a beginning, a fair journey ahead, and — most importantly, perhaps — the wonder and sense of discovery of a child looking upon nature in his earliest days.

The boat is emerging from a cavern, reminiscent somewhat — though much humbler in its proportions — of the great arched portal dividing Eden from the wilderness in *The Expulsion*. Cole in his poem, having assured us that his Dante-like passage through "the ancient shadowy woods" is no dream, describes this "wall / Of rock stupendous . . . a gray mountainous heap":

> . . . shadows fell from wild
> Portentous clouds that ever restlessly
> Hid the far summits from the wondering eye.
>
> And in the bosom of that stoney pile
> Which seemed the ruin of a shattered world
> Heaped skyward by some Titan's mighty toil
> A cavern yawned like death and changeful curled
> Across its sombre arches vast and wide
> Pale spectral mists; as though its awful depths to hide.
>
> But yet the eye unwilling to be barred
> Pierced far within the antre's silent womb,
> Arch beyond arch with many a fissure scarred,
> Perceived, until impenetrable gloom
> Sealed unto human vision, human thought
> The secret things with which its depths were fraught.

---

8 Noble, *Life and Works*, 211.
9 Tymn, *Thomas Cole's Poetry*, 146.

From the mysterious bosom of that cave
A gentle river took its winding way,
Reflecting freshly in the crystal wave
Rocks, sky and herbage which the glancing ray
Of the uprising sun made rosy light:
A wreath of glory on the dewy verge of night.

There is a lot to unpack in these few lines, which provide some insight into Cole's concept. First, as mentioned in the previous chapter, we have an echo—which, in my opinion, is intentional—of the opening cantos of Dante's *Commedia*. Cole is in a dark wood, and he comes upon a "stoney pile" in which "a cavern yawned like death," a cavern which proves to be a gateway. Dante likewise came from a dark wood and, with Virgil his guide, passed through a great gateway which was the entrance to hell. Beyond that portal Dante and Virgil descended to Acheron, the river of death, where they encountered Charon, the ferryman who ushers souls to their doom in the boat he pilots. Cole inverts all this in the description of his first scene of *Voyage*. As noted above, his own soul is his guide in a way reminiscent of the role Virgil plays for Dante—though (and this is an important difference, I believe) this implies an Emersonian self-reliance in Cole's poem instead of a reliance on outside assistance. Cole, in other words, trusts his intuition, his inner guide. It is, in a sense, for him what the Angel is for the Soul in *Voyage*. Whereas Dante and Virgil enter through the door to hell and come to a *river* and *boatman* that signify *death* and eternal *loss*, Cole alludes to the cavern in his painting as "like death"; but, in fact, both the river and the Angel who pilots the boat are death's converse: "That river of dark source / Is named the 'Stream of *Life*.'" Instead of going *into* the dark cave, as Dante and Virgil do, the infant Soul emerges *from it* joyously. Instead of grim Charon, the ferryman, piloting the vessel, we have the benign Angel.

Not only does Cole invert the imagery of Dante, but he inverts to some extent the imagery of *The Expulsion*. The movement of the latter was from the viewer's right to the viewer's left—Adam and Eve exiting Eden to the right, with its green and blue and rose hues, toward the wild, stormy, dark wilderness on the left. In the first scene of *Voyage*, the Soul is exiting the gloom and darkness on the viewer's left and entering what looks very much like an Edenic creation to the viewer's right. That there is to be a dark and tempestuous passage later for the voyaging Soul (in the third scene), we know. But in this very first scene, Cole is indicating that Eden and childhood are indistinguishable — every soul, in other words, is born innocent and with the innate capacity to wonder. It is an immature, unformed, imperfect stage in human life, but it is every person's individual "Eden." It is also the paradise we must inevitably leave behind if we are to become that for which we were created. "The fall" comes to each of us as life progresses. None of us begins as already "fallen"; rather *we* fall individually as we proceed, so that we might rise to something greater in the longer run.

The cave also implies a profound, impenetrable, indeed apophatic mystery to Cole. Its "bosom" is "mysterious." It has "awful depths to hide" and "secret things with which its depths were fraught." It is a "silent womb" — thus alluding to birth, of course — but it is inset in what appears like "the ruin of a shattered world." This is, perhaps, the closest we come in Cole's vision to a suggestion that it is the world that is in some sense "fallen." If so, it is into a "fallen" *environment* that the *innocent* human being is born. What's "fallen" — if "fallen" is even the best analogy — is the context in which the Soul finds himself; and yet the world he enters, reflected in his open-armed delight (or is the paradisial world Cole depicts a reflection of the Soul's delight?), shows no outwards trace, at least not yet, of a "fall." The mystery of the cave, though, is a great one, as the poem indicates. What, Cole seems to be wondering, is the origin from which the whole of nature, the world, and each one of us, in all our uniqueness, springs? Via the womb, it goes without saying, but the origin of "the Stream of Life" goes much deeper and further back than a single womb: "Arch beyond arch with many a fissure scarred," far beyond "human vision, human thought." There is more than just a hint of apophaticism in what Cole expresses here.

He seems to be acknowledging the fact that life and consciousness are inexplicable, their origin undiscoverable by human intellect. Human knowledge cannot reach that far, much less grasp it. Faith as an inward confidence, or what Kierkegaard called "infinite resignation," has something to impart to us of value, without using many or even any words. Philosophical, metaphysical, and theological speculations, on the other hand, involve countless words but say little of reliable value at the end of the day.[10] Cole might have agreed with

10 "For what seriousness can possibly remain in debating philosophical propositions that will never make an appreciable difference to us in action? And what would it matter, if all propositions were practically indifferent, which of them we should agree to call true or which false?" William James, *The Varieties of Religious Experience*, Lecture XVIII, "Philosophy"; p. 399 in The Library of America edition.

the last line of Wittgenstein's *Tractatus*: "What we cannot speak about we must pass over in silence"; or the opening line of the *Tao Te Ching*: "The Tao that can be told of is not the Absolute Tao; the Names that can be given are not Absolute Names."[11] For Cole, quite simply, the origin would be the answer his Christian faith supplied: God. But God is a mystery, not an "Absolute Name" (there is no such thing in any of our vocabularies), "with awful depths to hide."

Still, despite its limitations, Cole's inner guide tells him that "human thought, thanks be to God, can soar / Triumphant on the wings of light divine / And take its flight above the Shadow hoar."[12] He reminds himself and us that every human being is a mystery to himself or herself, and the implication is that that is how it should be. Once again, there is the suggestion, along the lines of Keats, that we are all passing through a "vale of Soul-Making." We must be content not only to regard God as a mystery, then, but our own selves as well. He reminds us that even Jesus had to travel "the Stream of Life" as we do:

> "Thou wert such infant Voyager, all men
> Have been—the thousands yet unborn will be
> Cast in such mould and of such origin
> Mysterious to themselves and even he
> Who bore our sorrows; for us shed his blood
> Was launched in that strange Bark and sailed the mystic flood . . ."[13]

This rare mention (rare, that is, for Cole) of the bond between every human soul and the person, sufferings, and death of Jesus is certainly a reminder to us of Cole's Christian faith. But what he emphasizes as constituting that bond is shared humanity. Jesus, like us, had to trust that his passage through this life, all his pains and trials, had meaning and, beyond the sepulcher, vindication. Gethsemane and Golgotha precede resurrection.

There is one last difference between *The Expulsion* and *Voyage* to be noted. Whereas in the former there is a clear division between Eden on one side of the great arch and the wilderness on the other, in *Voyage*—especially in the first two scenes—we see paradise and wilderness occupying the same world. The river will pass through both the bucolic and the sublime in the four scenes. The tranquil and the turbulent, peace and danger, blessing and threat will all be encountered as the Soul moves from infant delight to youthful

11 Ludwig Wittgenstein, *Tractatus Logico-Philosophicus*, trans. D. F. Pears and B. F. McGuiness (London and New York: Routledge, 1974), 7. *Tao Te Ching*, Chap. 1 (trans. Lin Yutang's, adapted slightly).

12 Tymn, *Thomas Cole's Poetry*, 147.

13 Ibid.

(over-)confidence, to adult anguish, and finally to the serenity of resigned old age. *The Expulsion*'s "either/or" scenario is replaced by *Voyage*'s "both/and." The tragic world doesn't stand in sharp contrast to earthly paradise; rather, both the tragic and the paradisial intermingle in our lives. The world through which we travel isn't simply "fallen" and evil; it is what we know it to be — an unpredictable environment where both good and evil coexist. And if the child in the boat is meant to reveal by his outstretched hands both immediate joy and the prospect of troubles ahead, then we have another emblem of the mixed existence Cole presents in these paintings.

Cole's allegory — even the accommodating Angel in the scenes — isn't meant to comfort us, but to disclose something true and relatable. The river moves in just one direction in all our lives: that's of the essence. The child has much to endure along the way, of which he is at the beginning blissfully ignorant, although in time he will invite trouble through culpable ignorance (as the next scene in the series will show). The same can be said of every one of us who recalls his or her childhood in perspective with the lives we have lived since. The child's delight is fleeting, of the moment: "The infant lives in the present. It neither looks back into the past, nor forward into the future." It's the closest to Eden we see in *Voyage*. Significantly, it's a picture of immaturity and cluelessness. "A higher destiny" than Eden, as Cole puts it in the poem, is what awaits the Soul in the end — or should be what awaits him, if he learns and grows rightly. Innocence, as beautiful as it is, isn't to be equated in quality with maturity or perfection. The latter, as Cole knows, is the objective, the "river of life" — the milieu for our inner growth — is its trajectory.

We may find the idea of life in this world as a "vale of Soul-Making" — we might prefer instead to call it "soul-forming" or "soul-developing" — problematic as a hypothesis. It has been ably updated and argued for philosophically and theologically in modern times, however, and it has its appeal still.[14] It isn't my intention here to argue for it, except to say that — whatever philosophical opinion we may hold regarding it — *it is, at least, based on a clearsighted view of this world as it is*. In other words, it has empirical foundation: the world really is a mix of good and evil, joy and anguish; children truly are born innocent and not guilty; our lives really do progress in recognizable stages; we are all headed in the direction of death and what lies beyond it; all that exists — including all

14 Most notably, it has been proposed by the late John Hick, British philosopher and theologian, especially in his book, *Evil and the God of Love* (1966), but also in such works as *Death and Eternal Life* (1976) and elsewhere.

life and the unlikely reality we call "consciousness" — emerges from a profound mystery... And so on. There is no reason why we should exclude the idea of God (or Brahman or the Tao or the Oversoul or whatever name we prefer to give to the greatest mystery) or the idea that our existence has meaning. We could do far worse than to accept the course of our lives in faith (or "infinite resignation") and apply ourselves to growing into truly human maturity.

This was an essential element of Cole's sacred vision and of his view of Christianity as well. It comes nearer, we could say, to the Eastern Christian understanding of our ultimate goal as "deification," rather than the Western concept of redemption. In the former view, we are meant "to become by grace what Christ is by nature." Cole may not have used such language or consciously held such a concept, but what we see in *The Voyage of Life* suggests that he understood something similar to that concept to be true. The innocent infant Soul must journey into his unpredictable future, and in the process be transformed. Innocence isn't the goal, but the starting point. Innocence is only an absence, after all — the infant's "views and capacities are limited to a very small circle." His life, through the arduous voyage of life still ahead of him, is meant to expand indefinitely that small, limited circle in which he exists. His true capacity is to coinhere with that supreme circle whose center is everywhere and circumference nowhere.

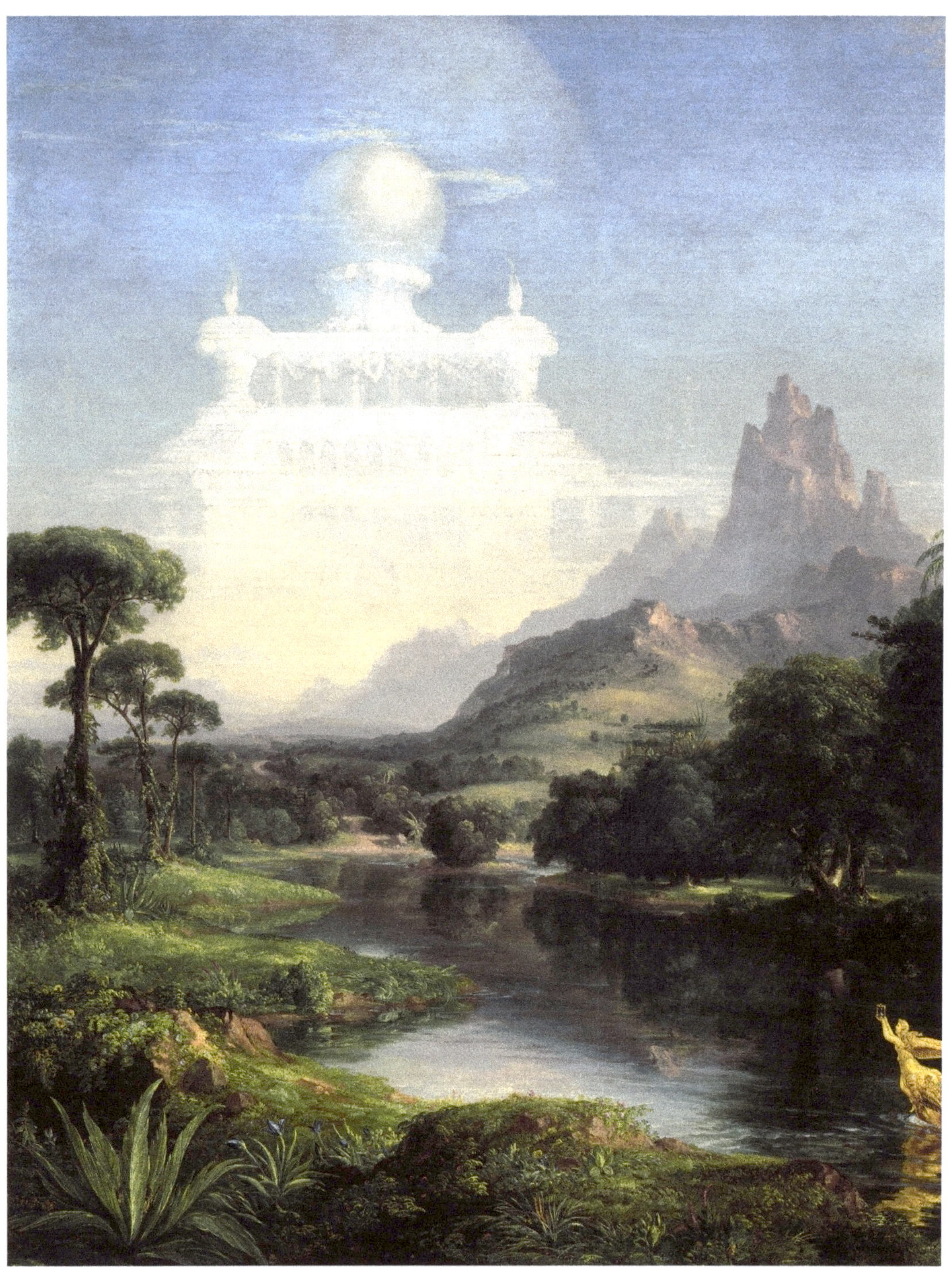

"YOUTH," DETAIL

IV. "Youth"

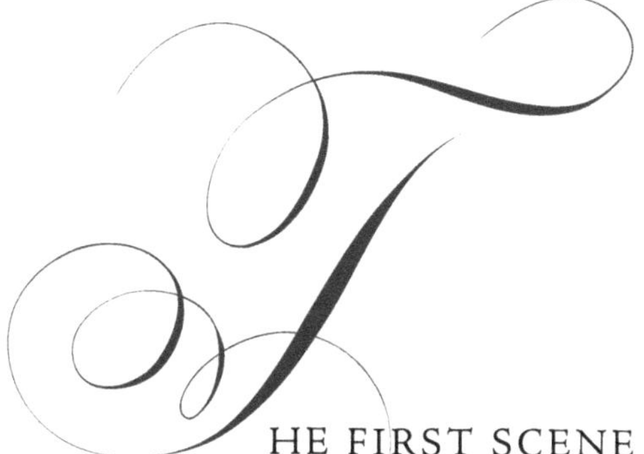

HE FIRST SCENE of *The Voyage of Life* depicted guileless, guiltless *innocence*. The second scene depicts *ignorance*. And although innocence is one state of ignorance, it isn't the only one. The typical person outgrows infantile innocence in a short span of time, usually well within the first few years. But even after innocence has started to show signs of giving way not only to a rapidly growing self-awareness, but also to selfishness and other less than appealing behaviors, ignorance still is evident. With education comes the paradox of "educated ignorance"—not infrequently a stage that lasts well into the early decade or two of adulthood. It is "educated ignorance" that Cole addresses in the painting of "Youth," the Soul as a young adult.

At the same time, as we shall see, the scene as described by the poem also lays stress on the theme of *wisdom*. What educated ignorance lacks is precisely that, and without its acquisition the youth will not reach his full humanity in this life. That may sound somewhat harsh, but it is what Cole intends for his work's viewers to understand and contemplate. The meaning of life's voyage, as Cole states straightforwardly in his poem, is for the purpose of gaining wisdom.

The second scene, then, in stark contrast to the dark, tempestuous one that will follow, presents us with a sunlit noonday landscape. Its predominant colors are azure, gold, mauve, rose, lush greens, and ivory for the grand illusory structure we see rising above the horizon, beyond the mountains, its Oriental dome among the clouds. As Cole described the scene, "The stream flows from the beholder, stretching far away directly towards a visionary pile

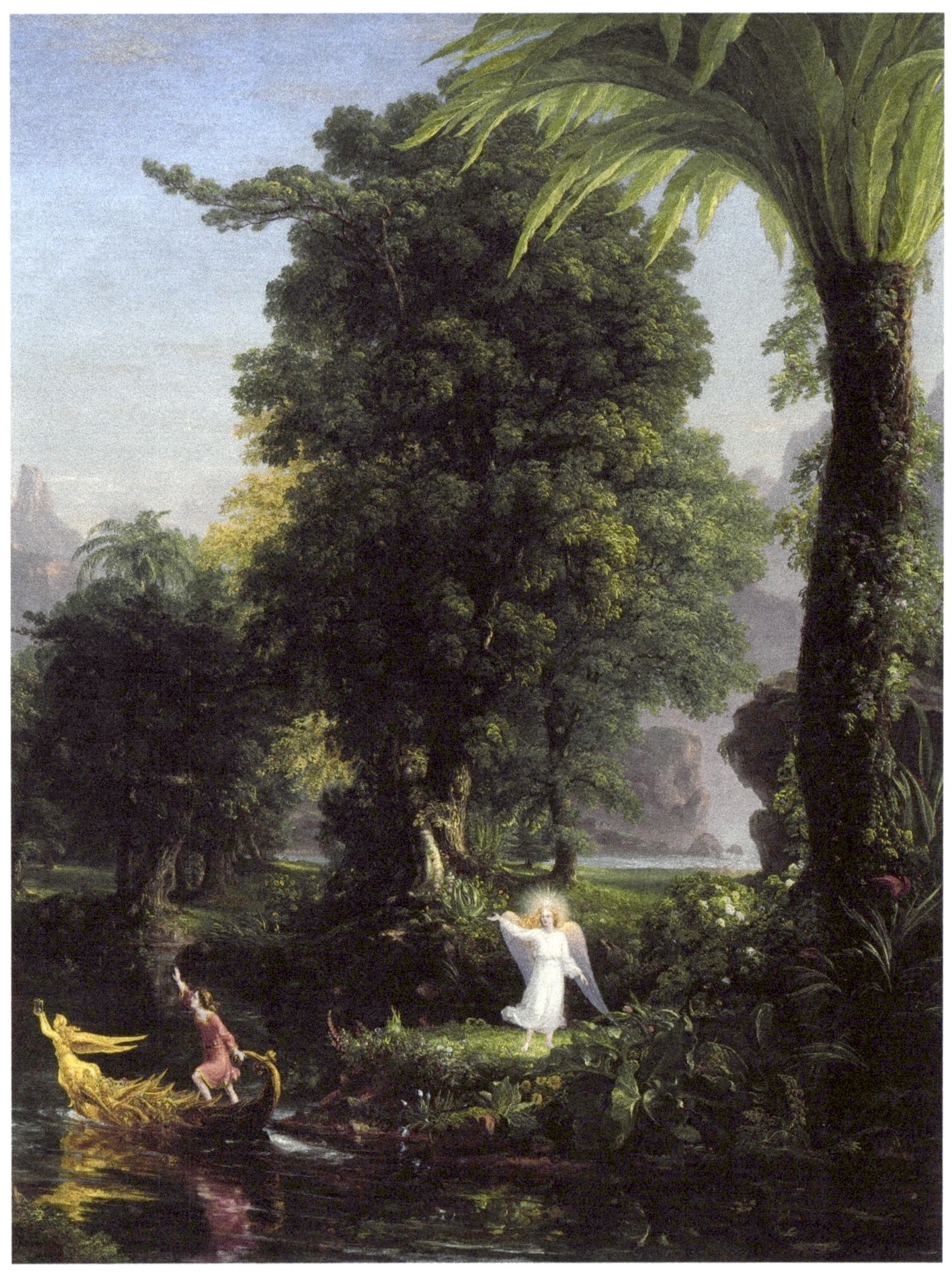

"YOUTH," DETAIL

of architecture, suspended in the air over the horizon."[1] And Cole indeed depicts the stream as flowing toward the "visionary pile"—but it only does so for a while. A bend ahead causes the water to veer toward the right, away from the direction where the illusion is seen. A path on land appears to lead toward the far-off vision. The youth in the boat, however, seems too preoccupied with the beguiling sight to notice the upcoming deviation in the river's course. Beyond the bend, the viewer who looks closely can see that the river snakes its way into the far distance, only to be lost to view between—ominously, as the next scene will reveal—great crags that loom over what becomes a swift, unruly current. The youthful Soul is taking leave of his Angel and assuming the tiller for himself. He is, as we have noted, *ignorant* of the fact that he's chasing after a fantasy (as we will learn), and all too eager to tackle the voyage without his Angel's assistance (or, as the youth might conceivably see it, her interference).

Cole informs us in the poem that the Soul here is "on manhood's verge, his eye / Flashing with confidence and hot expectancy."[2] He is no longer the innocent "fair Infant of my earlier dream." Unlike those fleeing figures of Adam and Eve in *The Expulsion from the Garden of Eden* described in the previous chapter, he is shown departing "Eden" of his own volition. As Cole describes it, "His hand had grasped the helm once gently held / By that Angelic figure so serene."[3] The youthful Soul, in effect, brushes aside his Angel to take the rudder. He wants his independence. He no longer feels any need for the Angel's guidance. He asserts his autonomy, perhaps demands it as his right. The Angel, on the other hand, ever gracious, doesn't contend with him. She allows the brush-off and gives the boat over to his control: ". . . the Angel stood / Upon the bank as from the Boat just freed / And waved her graceful hand and bade the Youth 'God Speed.'"[4] Despite being slighted by the youth's pride, she takes the offense in stride, without contention, and lets him go his way.

The upshot is that he is destined, by his own decision, to learn the hard way. That's how it must be and, as Cole indicates in the poem, this risky prospect was not unexpected by the Angel. This stage was, in fact, inevitable. And of course, the youth cannot stay in his Eden. The river, remember, is the river of time. It must move on, and he must travel on it. That's how life is. He has no choice in the matter, no decision to make—he must proceed on. His

---

1 From a letter. Noble, *Life and Works*, 212.

2 Tymn, *Thomas Cole's Poetry*, 153.

3 Ibid., 151.

4 Ibid.

mistake does not lie in the fact that he fails to recognize the city in the sky to be an illusion, or that he fails to see the bend in the river ahead—again, he has no choice but to ride out the river's course; rather, his mistake is leaving his Angel behind. And, it seems to be Cole's suggestion, that's the mistake we all make, too. It's not too much to say, then, that the Angel is, as the multivalent metaphorical figure she is, an image of wisdom.

So, everything from this point on revolves around the acquisition of *divine wisdom*. This goal—the Soul's getting of wisdom—is for Cole the true purpose of God's providence at work in human life; and the Soul in the series, as we know, represents every person's earthly journey. Providence is operative at every stage of the Soul's pilgrimage in *Voyage*. If we miss that aspect of the series, we miss the most essential one. It is providence that drives him "through hell and high water" (to borrow an old but apt phrase) toward wisdom's attainment. We need to bear that governing idea in mind throughout *Voyage*, the last scene of which will be not only one of old age, self-surrender, and death, but a vision also of wisdom providentially achieved and rewarded.

Wisdom is the supreme attribute in earthly existence, the most valuable acquisition in a person's life. Procuring it entails the humbling of pride, and humbling comes by way of one's actual experiences in life—including such disagreeable but very human ones as making poor decisions and suffering the consequences, disappointments, losses, moral failings, remorse, enduring evils of every variety, and so on. Without entirely realizing what he's doing, betrayed by an apparition of his own mind's devising (the city in the clouds), the youth presumptuously dismisses the guide of his higher intellect and makes his exit out of "Eden." Cole makes the comparison of the scene's landscape with Eden explicit in the poem:

> Again I raised my downcast eyes to look
> Upon the scene so beautiful when lo!
> The stream no longer from the cavern took
> Its gentle way 'tween flowery banks and low
> But through a landscape varied, rich and vast
> Beneath a sky that dusky cloud had surely never passed . . .
>
> And trees like those which spread their pleasant shade
> O'er the green slopes of Eden, and the bowers
> Of the once sinless pair, soft, intermingling made

Stood on each shore with branches lifted high
And caught eolian strains that wandered from the sky.[5]

The Soul, then, recapitulates Adam and Eve's loss of paradise. But there is a difference. Whereas Adam and Eve, because of their disobedience, were forcefully expelled, the youth in the painting takes his own leave. His separation from the Angel and departure can't precisely be called an act of outright disobedience, but the attentive viewer knows it's a reckless act notwithstanding. If nothing else, that bend in the river, which the youth doesn't notice, signifies he will soon be heading in a wildly divergent direction for which he was not prepared. Cole, as we recall from the last chapter, didn't embrace the classical Western Christian notion of "original sin," with its inherited guilt, but he did believe that there is some inborn tendency that bends us toward "sin," a bent common to all human beings. This is what he illustrates for us here. The youth's "sin," to put it succinctly, is to act in ignorance. Cole's idea of congenital sin is thus different from the "classical" (Augustinian) one, but it is a perceptive one. It isn't burdened with abstract definitions, but it is based on what is empirically observable in human behavior. We could say Cole's is an existential interpretation, not a doctrinally systematic one; it is a more "poetic" view of the matter than a "prosaic" one.

There is the possibility that Cole was aware of biblical words and their etymologies and shaped the visual metaphors of this scene accordingly. The words traditionally translated as "sin" ("wrongdoing," "offense," etc.) mean "missing the mark" (both the Hebrew *cheit* and the Greek *hamartia* mean just that) or "going off-course." The crucial moment when the Soul goes woefully "off-course" in the series is when he chooses to leave the company of his Angel, no longer letting her steer and guide him. He will inevitably face the consequences of this separation. To all appearances, he does not act from any malice toward the Angel, but in bidding her adieu he does act in ignorance. It's his overconfident ignorance that is guaranteed to cause him his ensuing grief. But we should also note that the Angel is gracious—she is not the forbidding angel barring the gates of Eden behind him. There is no flaming sword.

Cole, however, doesn't leave us with the impression that the Soul's bad choice is an irremediable disaster. Instead, it seems to have been destined to happen, given human nature, for which providence—as the word implies—has made provision in advance. Indeed, Cole seems to imply that the youth's decision

5 Ibid., 149.

is a "felix culpa"—a "happy" or fortuitous "fault"—provided that, in the long run, it drives him toward wisdom's attainment.

This thought takes us back, then, to the idea of "educated ignorance." "Eden," we have indicated, is a condition or state in a person's development. It had that import in the painting of the infant Soul. It begins as an immature state of innocence and openness, but—as knowledge accumulates (analogous, perhaps, with the mythical Tree of the Knowledge of Good and Evil)—it becomes an "educated ignorance." The infant Soul was harmless, wide-eyed, delighted, open. In his Edenic condition, he was merely unformed, undeveloped. Most of us retain vague recollections of such a brief period in our own lives, half dreamlike, half vivid memories. Each of us once lived in a personal "Eden," from which we have "fallen." In the infant's case, "innocence" was *only* the absence of acquired knowledge, a condition neither good nor bad. He was the axiomatic "blank slate." He could make no claim to positive morality, even though he was guiltless and sinless.[6]

Innocence, with the acquisition of knowledge, is soon lost, and "educated ignorance" supplants it. We should, of course, be especially well acquainted with that paradoxical fact of life in our Western civilizational societies.[7] By "educated" in this case I do not mean the gaining of hands-on practical knowledge, but rather the rote learning of information that our "advanced" culture tends to equate with knowledge. We can correctly assume that the youth in Cole's

6 We might see in this an inversion of the idea that "the knowledge of good and evil" was bad for Adam and Eve in the Genesis story. Much could be said about this (especially about the ancient story itself and what it would have meant within its Middle Eastern mythological context), but suffice it to say that, even in classical Christian interpretation, "the sin of Adam and Eve" wasn't the mere acquisition of knowledge, which they would have received in due time anyway, but the impulsive way by which it was appropriated. Knowledge, it should be noted, can only be handled rightly by someone possessing wisdom—which is a point that Cole seems to be making in the series. We should not lose sight that the idea of the "felix culpa" is an ancient one in Christian thought, and, in one form or another, Cole would likely have been familiar with it.

7 I doubt that this same assumption applies to indigenous peoples who have managed, usually against the odds and much outward pressure, to maintain their own cultures and ways of life. What our civilization has elevated to the highest rung on the ladder of "knowledge"—along with its forms of schooling, often inflicted by well-meaning "civilized" peoples on indigenous peoples—has often had very little relevance to their survival, traditions, and understanding of what it means to be human. The consequences for those cultures have often been less than entirely beneficial, to say the least. Cole assumes modern civilization as the norm, though not uncritically, as his *The Course of Empire* shows. His sympathy for the lost "wildness" of the Native American world is also evident in his work, as judged by the standards of his age.

scene, given that he is a modern Western young adult, has gone through his obligatory schooling. Now he is eager to launch out on his own and prove himself, equipped with his education. He wants to be unhampered by what he regards as his over-protective guide. He is ignorant of what life will throw at him, but he's self-assured in his sense of his own knowledge. Ignorance is like that. Alexander Pope's observation that "a little learning is a dangerous thing" might be applicable in this case. Ignorance and knowledge, in other words, are not at odds.

The youth's "dismissal" of his Angel reminds us, as Cole probably intended it should, of a young person who leaves home with the presumption that he knows better and maybe more than his elders do. The Angel indulges him, not clinging to him, not protecting him (she is not a "helicopter Angel"!), seemingly knowing that unless the Soul undergoes true and even painful learning—gaining true knowledge of the world and, most importantly, of himself in the bargain—he will have no opportunity of growing into maturity. (All reasonable parents can probably recognize this familiar scenario.) The Soul's development will only happen over the course of years and decades, through experience. His immature fantasies will be dispelled. What and who he is in his essence is what he will *become* in the process, not what he was in his infantile innocence. He will only come to know himself, in so far as it can be known in this life, as it develops. It will take years. Only when he is able to see where he has been and what he has come through will he attain a firmer idea of his identity, and then it may not prove to be at all what he imagined it was in his youth. But the youth is not at that point yet. In the meantime, life's exigencies will hone and whittle him down to the person that's in the process of emerging from his unshaped substance. There is, of course, always the possibility that a person will not learn from his or her experience. Many never do in this life. But the lack of developing self-awareness will result in a stunted maturity, one frequently plagued by bitterness, anger, disappointment, discontent, a general lack of peace, and other ills.

What is lacking in one's puerile "educated ignorance," as we said, is *wisdom*. For it to bud, there must be experience. That's the fertilizer. Wisdom's most vital quality is humility. The wise person knows and can freely admit his or her ignorance; knowledge is thereby tempered by sensitivity and a recognition of its incompleteness. Wisdom, because it is essentially humble, abhors unnecessary contention (like the Angel), doesn't have a need to show off, doesn't boast, and can tolerate ambiguity and the gray areas of life. Once allowed to take root, budding wisdom incrementally transforms the educated ignoramus into an evolving soul. A little leaven will leaven the whole lump. It is the essential need of the Soul and what his voyage is really all about. As Cole's "soul" informs him in the poem:

> "Shrouded as now thou art in earth
> Thou canst not see the [true] end for which came mortal birth."
>
> "In the Almighty mind the secret cause is laid . . ."
>
> "*Wisdom is born of sorrow and of care*
> And from man's conflicts with the world arise
> A sense of weakness and of chilling fear
> And driven from earth his hopes ascend the skies.
> Thus he is launched upon the stream alone
> To chasten pride and give young desire a holier tone . . ."[8]

Note the word "desire" in the last line of the stanza above. What does Cole mean by giving the Soul's "desire a *holier* tone"? As the third of the four scenes will make evident, the getting of that "tone" will take a heavy toll on him. He will be stripped down. His desires will become less and less, even as the boat's accouterments and decorations are demolished by the rocks and rapids. With that line, the poem has alerted us that we are to regard this deceivingly idyllic second scene as a sham.

Unsurprisingly perhaps, I have seen this scene, separated from the rest of the series, sometimes framed, sometimes used on social media, misleadingly displayed for the purpose of personal inspiration. After all, with our cultural predilection for positive thinking, the scene seems to fit contemporary sensibilities with an apparently chipper motivational message. Its glowing dream-city looks a bit like the Taj Mahal—and everybody loves inspirational pictures of the Taj Mahal. It hovers there among the clouds in an azure sky above a flowery, paradisial landscape. The starry-eyed young adult below stretches out toward the marvelous horizon and a beckoning future. The cheerful Angel waves bye-bye as the boy embarks on his journey toward his fantastic destination. The scene comes across, upon shallow viewing, like an invitation to

8 Tymn, *Thomas Cole's Poetry*, 153. Emphasis added. I might add here the observation that the wisest *children* I have ever known were those who were terminally ill and had no chance of growing up or "developing" over the course of a more extended lifetime. In my experience, they were more developed, more mature in wisdom, than the majority of adults I have known, except for those who have lived to great age.

"follow your dream," or an illustration that should have some legend attached to it like "be what you want to be." But as we know, the river doesn't lead to the wondrous city, and even though the scene is bathed in dazzling noonday light, it is a deceptive light. The Oz-like vision is a mirage, a humbug, without substance, unreal. In short, the scene is the antithesis of an inspirational, motivational meme. Its razor-sharp point is that reality will not be denied. Up ahead are looming rocks and turbulent rapids. They can't be evaded. There is no straight, easy route to where "The palace stands [just] beyond, reached by a gentle slope."[9] The bend in the river will take the Soul on a route he has not anticipated. His insubstantial desires will, consequently, be forced to change, be shredded, or shed, and—under duress—he will develop new, more apposite, ones. The Soul will know "weakness and . . . chilling fear," "sorrow and . . . care."

Those are unpleasant, even depressing, realities that the Soul—and we are right if we see that they apply to us all—will undergo. We don't like to contemplate such things. But is any life ever entirely devoid of them? More to the point, empirically speaking, is it possible to evolve into a mature human being without learning from experiencing them? The answer depends on what we consider a "mature human being" to be. For Cole, yet again, it means to become *wise*—"the end for which came mortal birth." Another way to put it, this time in Cole's own theological idiom, since "in the Almighty mind the secret cause is laid," to be fully human means ultimately to share in the divine nature.[10] Wisdom, not cleanliness, is next to godliness.

Thus, the Angel relinquishes the helm of the boat to the Soul, who sets out alone. The separation of the two characters looks ominous. If, as I suggested above, the Angel in some sense is the Soul's own spiritual intelligence, his "higher self"—just as Cole's own soul in the poem is his "higher self," his guide, interpreter, and interlocutor—the suggestion here might be that the Soul has lost touch with this aspect of his nature, that there is an inner disjunction. Or, put differently, part of him is no longer listening to "the still, small voice" within. He has silenced his intuition, his capacity to see the big picture. The spirit has been crowded out by competing "voices," other ideas, other desires—as Cole puts it, what he has set his mind on is "the tempting semblance of a conqueror's crown / And wreath to bind the brows of him

---

9 Ibid., 152.

10 ". . . Whereby are given unto us exceeding great and precious promises: that by these ye might be partakers of the divine nature, having escaped the corruption that is in the world . . ." (2 Peter 1:4)

who wins renown."[11] He has conceitedly let his ego run loose. I believe we are correct to see this inner disjunction as an interpretation of the scene. We are all inwardly divided, in need of reintegration, of being made whole, in short, in need of wisdom.

But the separation is also more apparent than real. The Angel will not absent herself entirely from the voyaging Soul, even if her presence is hidden from him. She will be—as Cole's third scene will show—still at work "behind the scenes."

> He is alone; but still deserted never
> The Angel yet shall watch his perilous way;
> And though the clouds of earth may seem to sever,
> Still through the darkness shines the Angelic ray;
> And in the hour of midnight o'er the deep
> The Guardian Spirit kind will constant vigil keep.[12]

The mention of "midnight o'er the deep" in the verse above refers to the final scene of the series, which will be that of the hour of death. Only then will there be a reunion of the Soul, now grown old, with his Angel. It will come in darkness at the culmination of the voyage, where the stream of life runs into the vast ocean. The ocean, like the cavern in the first scene, represents the great mystery that is both our origin and our end. But the sea is distant in this second scene, far ahead in the youth's future, and he can't even imagine it at this stage. What he has only just embarked on is beyond his comprehension.

There is something wistful about this scene, under its bright surface, especially if we have grown old ourselves and can see in it something of our own youth. Or, perhaps, we see our children in it, or maybe even our grandchildren. With all its cheerful colors and noonday light, there is still a melancholy to it. If we are old enough, it may conjure up memories of old hopes, old visions we once had. Some goals we set for ourselves in life we might even have reached. But we likely never saw coming what else came into our lives unbidden—the losses, the deaths, the fractured relations, the sicknesses, the sorrows, the desperate times, the ways we hurt others or hurt ourselves, the trials that came upon us by accident or nature or malice, and so on. A list of miseries and troubles can get monotonous. Like the youth,

---

11 Tymn, *Thomas Cole's Poetry*, 152.

12 Ibid., 153.

though, most of us never paid much attention to the upcoming bends or the looming rocks downriver. We took our chances, and most of us did let go of "the better angels of our nature" at some juncture in our lives and only reunited with them — assuming we ever did — after much too long a time.

All this Cole evokes in this deceptively sunny scene, when we look at it in line with what follows. And it is what follows that rightly gives the scene its proper context, and also its poignancy and power.

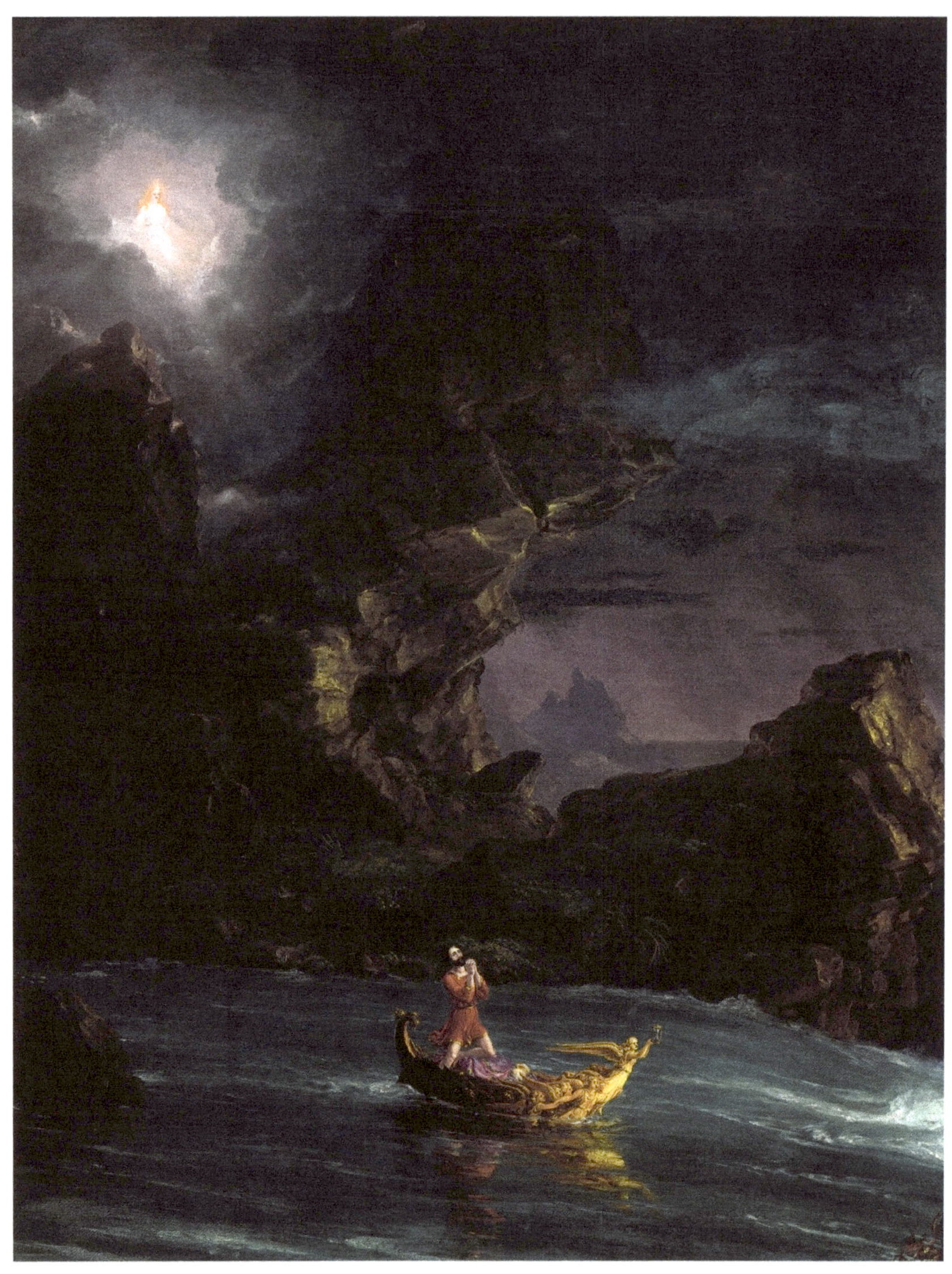

"MANHOOD," DETAIL

V. "Manhood"

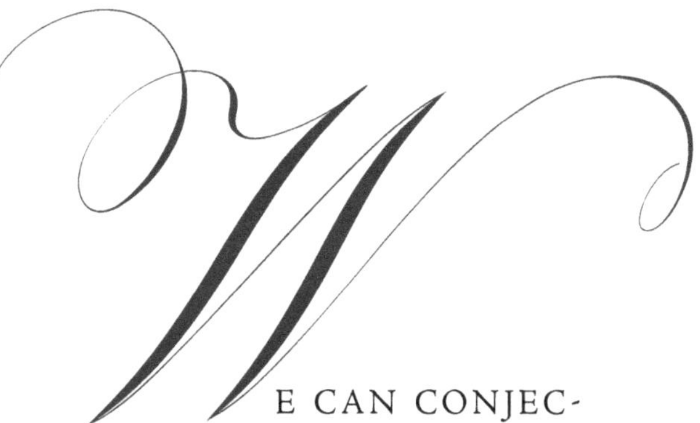

E CAN CONJECTURE how much the series was, for Cole, autobiographical in some way. The fact that it was a work he prized during the brief remainder of his life says that he may well have regarded it as such. The poem is written, as we have seen, in the first person, in which his own soul instructs him concerning the meaning of it, applying it directly to himself. Undoubtedly, he saw his own life reflected in the scenes. As we noted in the second chapter above, his life seems to have been lived without a great deal of drama or upheaval. Yet we can surmise that he had his fair share of struggles—financial worries, doubts, fears, and so on—about which the record we have is silent. Although the series is about the general human condition, we must assume it is also an allegory that grows out of his own experience and his peculiarly sensitive nature. With that muted background in mind, then, we come to the third scene of the set.

It is the crucial stage of the Soul's voyage. And *crucial* is, I believe, precisely the right word to describe it, and that for two related reasons. First, because we are—to switch briefly from Cole's grand analogy of a river—at a *cross*roads in the life of the Soul. Here is the *crucible*, in which he is to be reshaped, reformed, and inwardly reoriented: "This is the crisis—this is the decisive hour," Cole's soul explains to him in the poem.[1]

Cole does nothing to soften the impact of this scene in the poem. If anything, he intensifies it. Our contemporary sensibilities might regard the scene and Cole's poetic explanation as going a bit "over the top," too gloomy and negative in tone. We live, after all, in a different cultural epoch, one in which

---

1 Tymn, *Thomas Cole's Poetry*, 155.

many of us become profoundly uncomfortable by whatever doesn't present us with an unreserved affirmation of our self-perceptions and our wants or expects us to undertake serious self-critical introspection. We are more inclined in our age to demand what we assume we are entitled to as "free" individuals, and less inclined to scrutinize, investigate, and—if need be—dissect our deeply-held biases, half-baked notions, motivations, and intentions. Our age is fast-paced, noisy, with endless opportunities for distraction; hence it's not at all difficult to avoid exploring ourselves at much depth. We have instant entertainment with the push of a button. We can put on earphones and drown ourselves aurally, we can escape unpleasant "real reality" with Virtual Reality or by binge-watching television or immersing ourselves in gaming or mentally living in some franchise's fantasy "universe." That's our present age, which we take pretty much for granted (which is itself a problem—a sort of mental myopia). But what we take for granted would have been inconceivable in Thomas Cole's time. Critical introspection of a serious nature was far more common, as personal journals and letters of the period—common modes of self-expression, often written at great length and with much detail by our standards—attest. Even the composing of poetry, sometimes included in journal entries and missives, was a pastime engaged in by many who had no intention to publish.

Entertainment in the nineteenth century, at least for the better-educated classes, consisted mainly of reading or writing by lamp or candlelight (electricity became available more than half a century after Cole's death), or playing one's own musical instruments, or attending the theater, or playing outdoor or indoor games. When they weren't occupied in personal pursuits, quiet and reflective, they were engaged with others in conversation. It was literally a darker world, and it was a quieter world, unless one lived in the center of a city. There was not much in the way of escapism. Cole's favored hobby was hiking out in nature, often alone. Excursions were a treat, whether in company with others or not. (But it's a mistake perhaps to say that such engagement with the natural world is "escapism," since we know now how integral to health and sanity such exposure is. We are always poorer for the lack of it, psychologically especially, regardless of the age in which we live.) For those who were not as educated or well-off as those of Cole's class, distractions were fewer still and frequently rougher, more makeshift.

In sum, then, many of us today are less pensive, less engaged with others in our locale and immediate surroundings, less exposed to nature, and less exposed to the most unpleasant realities of life. For example, Cole and his contemporaries met with death under the same roof as themselves as a matter of course, even the deaths of the very young. Consequently, ongoing reflection on one's own mortality, even at an early age, was common. We, on the other hand, are constantly bombarded with enticements to look away and indulge in artificial escapism even as older adults. The sad result of this propensity is the evident emotional immaturity we can see among so many who are well into their adult years. As poet and novelist Jim Harrison wrote somewhere, "If everything becomes a diversion what is left at the center?" We could answer that in these days, looking at our society in general, not terribly much. We tend to flee our center and squander even the little time we have that might be better spent in quiet thought.

So, then, if Cole's third painting strikes us as excessively morbid or somber, which it did not do for viewers in previous generations, that's a reflection on both his age and ours. The real question for us is which age in the long run tended to see reality more clearly, without protective mental blinkers or the mechanisms for conjuring easy automated illusions. Cole may have clothed reality in allegory, but he wasn't engaged in escapism.[2] We can still recognize that his work depicts reality through its metaphors. He was, as we will see, applying his craft to criticism both of himself and of his work's viewers.

The second reason that this can be called the "crucial" scene of the series is because it mirrors in a few particulars the customary imagery used to depict Christ's Agony in Gethsemane. In other words, it is *crucial* because it points toward a sort of *crucifixion* of the adult Soul. We see him praying in the boat, much as Jesus is portrayed supplicating the Father in religious art. Shining down from above, we see the Angel, just as in some depictions of Christ's agony in the garden angels are shown attending him. Even in the dimly seen cloud above the vessel, a grim bearded figure can be descried bearing in his hand a chalice (more about this below), just as Jesus is sometimes shown being offered the chalice of his sufferings. Cole certainly seems to be echoing visually the Gethsemane motif. This, then, is the Soul's "agony," his way of the cross, his cup of sufferings. Cole knew that the appeal Jesus made to his disciples was that they should "take up" their "cross" and follow him. The Soul is precisely, then, depicted within the context of his own "decisive hour."

2 None of this, incidentally, is meant to overlook the real evils existing in Cole's day and his adopted nation. One need only consider such contemporary facts as slavery, the vicious treatment of Native Americans, the ravaging of natural resources, and the flagrant land-grabs by the United States of Mexican territories.

To appreciate better the painting, we should not bypass this visual allusion to a motif of standard Christian iconography.

As in all four paintings, what we see here is representative of the inner state of the Soul, of what is going on inside him as well as what is happening to him on the outside. The inner and the outer are not two distinct realities. They mirror one another.

First, what is occurring within his heart and mind reveals the impact on him of outward circumstances. This is, of course, true for all of us. What we experience in our minds, both that part of them that is alert during our wakeful hours but also the greater unconscious part of them that we can only dimly perceive when we are at our most self-aware, is always affected by what's going on in our outer life. The Soul in the painting is surrounded by the dangers and horrors of *deformed nature* and the *demonic*. On one level, these are meant to be understood as uncontrollable outside forces bearing down on the Soul. Second, though, these forces exist not only in that grisly external wilderness through which he is passing externally, which affect him inwardly; more importantly, the frenzied forces Cole depicts embody—that is to say, they make visible to us in the form of metaphors—the condition of the Soul's inner self. We should note here, too, that this is the resultant condition of the Soul who left the Angel behind in the previous scene. The Angel, of course, is not really absent even here, but the turmoil the man is undergoing reveals the disunity between them that he chose earlier.

We need to look more closely at the way Cole depicts both the *deformed natural scenery* and the *demonic*, since these reflect the Soul's condition. Regarding the disfigurement of the natural world visible in the painting, we first should note that Cole held to an idealistic view of what nature *should* be and what the degradation of nature did to its created perfection. His views in this regard reveal both the lifelong influence of Romanticism on his thought, which saw in nature the divine, and at the same time his Christian conviction that nature had been made "good" or perfect at the beginning. These two streams, Romanticism and Christian belief, were mutually influential in his age, and this was certainly the case in Anglicanism, which he had adopted.[3] So it is

3 Anglicanism was by no means the only church to be influenced by the amorphous and pervasive Romantic movement (perhaps "mood" might be a better label for it than "movement" in this case). We see its effects in the Catholicism of the period and in the various Protestant denominations and sects, as well, ranging from elevated poetry, art, and theology at the one extreme, to sentimental religious kitsch at the other.

we see in his journal entry of November 27, 1842, a significant clarification of his views about painting nature:

> By truth in nature, I mean anything's fulfillment of the objects and purposes for which it was created. The true leaf or flower, for instance, will be that which perfectly performs its various functions, and so accomplishes its appointed work . . . By the true in art, I mean the imitation of the true in nature, not the imitation of accidents, nor merely the common imitation of nature indiscriminately. *All nature is not true.* I may instance the withered vine, the imperfect flower, the stunted tree. *These are false, and deformities. I would say, the true and the beautiful in art are the reproduction of the perfect in nature,* and the carrying out of principles which nature suggests.[4]

In light of the above passage, we can suppose that the third scene of *The Voyage of Life* was intended to convey nature as ravaged, destroyed, imperfect, deformed, and the antithesis of "truth in nature" and therefore of "beauty." The painting can, of course, be considered a rendering of the "sublime," but Cole would almost certainly have balked at using the term "beautiful" to describe it. We can extend this idea, as well, to his rendering of the wilderness outside Eden in *The Expulsion*. This scene of ruination is the world the voyaging Soul has now entered; as mirroring his inner condition, we could turn this around and say it's also the world that has entered the Soul. The poem is unsparing in this regard: *the distorted nature in the scene parallels the distorted nature of the Soul himself.*

Cole describes the blasted landscape in terms intended to terrify: the voyager passes by a "dismal vale—"

> Its sides down stooping into night were bossed
> With jagged rocks—above huge crags rose pale
> And quivering in thick turbulent air
> Like hell-frighted spectres starting from their lair.
>
> It seemed the earthquake there had oped his jaws
> And fierce Convulsion rent the ribs of Earth . . .
>
> Onward [the river] dashed and with tyrannic force
> Swept o'er the fractured rocks and foamed and fell
> And reeled from side to side with thunders hoarse:

4 Noble, *Life and Works*, 251. Emphasis added.

Though broken off and baffled naught could quell: —
Athwart the steep the streaming floods did pour
And rocky fragments fell, dislodged amid the roar...

... the Boat was seen
Fleet as a meteor thwart the midnight deep.
Like famished wolves when the scared prey is nigh,
The pale demoniac floods roared louder as for joy...[5]

... And so on. In the painting, the turbulent clouds above are of dark smoky charcoal gray, turning to mauve with the declining sun. Greenish rushing white-capped rapids carry the boat along, and — above the waters and the voyager — a strange greenish-gray cloud is seen to hover ominously. The great crags are rusty brown, as are the autumn trees to the viewer's right, tossed and savagely rent by the tempest. The vessel is now bereft of its rudder, and the Soul is in a posture of supplication, hands clasped, praying for succor. Above the fray we see the bright Angel, serenely watching over the scene through the clouds, surrounded by heavenly light.

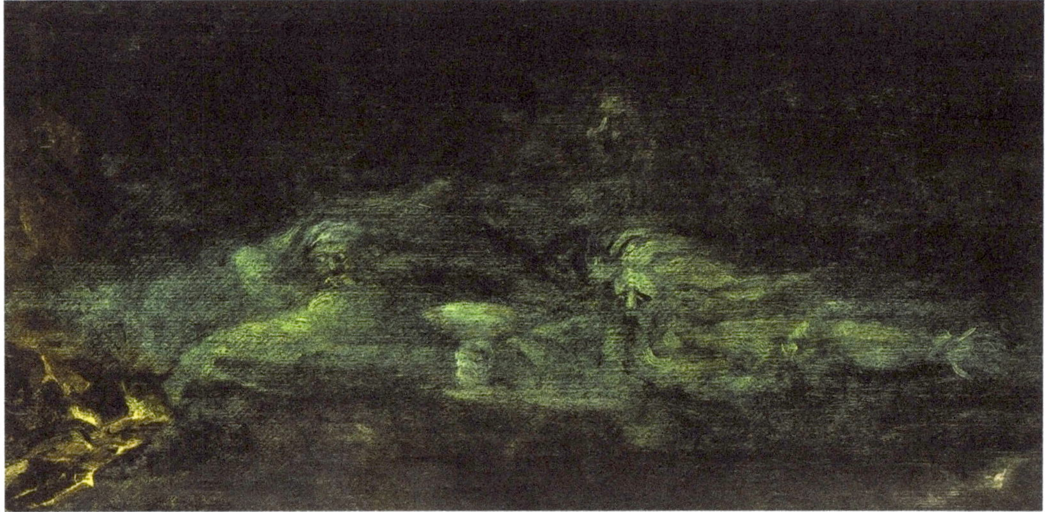

Coming back to that greenish-gray cloud hovering menacingly overhead, the viewer who looks closely will note that at least three murky figures combine to make up the manifestation. Woeful bearded faces, somewhat reminiscent of the many bearded figures in William Blake's art, glare down upon the

5 Tymn, *Thomas Cole's Poetry*, 154.

traveler. We can make out their outstretched arms and they appear to be swooping down, out of the dark overshadowing storm clouds. They clearly mean the Soul no good. The most prominent of these baleful figures extends his right arm and his hand clasps a cloud-formed chalice. Again, the Gethsemane motif seems to be invoked here, but this particular "cup of suffering" isn't of heavenly origin but emerges out of a markedly hellish one. If the visual association with Christ's Agony in the Garden signifies anything, it is that of Gethsemane inverted. The awful cup is not salvific but rather the opposite, malevolent in nature.

These figures, then, are Cole's rendering of the *demonic*. They possibly stand for the three trials, depicted in their demon forms, that he refers to in his poem as "Adversity," "Sorrow," and "Temptation" (see the pertinent verses two paragraphs below). In addition, Cole also mentions in the poem—not capitalized like the aforementioned three are—"estrangement [of friends]," and "sin." All these ills are traced back, as consequences, to the Soul's youthful—we might say "original"—presumptuousness. The demonic is alluded to a number of times in the poem: the rocks are like "hell-affrighted spectres," the region itself is "a den where demons had their birth," the floods are "demoniac," and the Angel all the while looks down upon the "Demon Shapes."[6] Indeed, the poem hints, this cloud of "demons" was the concealed reality behind that false vision of the city for which the youth had left the Angel in the previous scene. That vision has now entirely dissipated, revealing the true face(s) behind the deception for what they are.

The idea that demons are "invited in" by our actions is an old one. Whether or not Cole believed in the existence of literal demons is beyond my knowledge to say. Doubtless, he believed in incorporeal spirits, but he also associates the demonic with the common and tangible maladies of life—his "demons" are representative of the troubles of the spirit and the mind. As such, they are primarily oppressors of our thoughts. Cole may not have known that the link between "evil spirits" and "evil thoughts" goes far back into Christian literature, most notably back to monastic culture both East and West. The most germane of the monastic fathers in this regard was undoubtedly Evagrius of Pontus (AD 345–399), who, although he was viewed as an Origenist and therefore something of a heretic for centuries, nonetheless continued to be read by the orthodox, his name often concealed by attributing his writings to more

6 Tymn, *Thomas Cole's Poetry*, 154–55.

acceptable writers. His eight "evil thoughts," sowed by the demons (gluttony, fornication, avarice, anger, sadness, acedia,[7] vainglory, and pride) evolved over time to become what are called the seven "capital," "cardinal," or "deadly" sins (pride, greed, lust, envy, gluttony, wrath, and sloth—"thoughts" and urges which, in effect, lead to "actual" sin). Through John Cassian (AD 365–435) and others, Evagrius's thought entered the mainstream of Medieval monastic faith and practice, and through monasticism influenced the wider Church. As scholars have noted, there is psychological insight to be had among the more sophisticated Medieval spiritual writers who—as strange as it might sound to modern ears—took the subject of demons and their activities seriously, connecting them to what motivates thoughts, words, and deeds. "Evil spirits" or "evil breaths/winds" blow through our hearts, in-breathed (to use the essential analogy) from the world outside, prompting urges and notions in our minds that are unhealthy—think of a virus against which we must take precautions. What counters this unhealthy and pervasive spiritual miasma in Christian thought is the Holy Spirit ("holy breath/wind"), which purifies our impressionable thoughts. This understanding may not apply to Cole's mention of "Adversity" and "Sorrow," but it certainly would apply to his mentioning of "Temptation" and "sin." The idea of invasive "spirits" that require our interior "cleansing" by the Holy Spirit would have found an echo in a prayer no doubt quite familiar to Thomas Cole, which is said at the beginning of every Prayer Book service of Holy Communion:

> Almighty God, unto whom all hearts be open, all desires known, and from whom no secrets are hid; cleanse the thoughts of our hearts by the inspiration of thy Holy Spirit, that we may perfectly love thee, and worthily magnify thy holy Name; through Christ our Lord. *Amen.*

This was a reworked prayer with Medieval roots, and every phrase in it reflects its contemplative nature.[8]

---

7 Spiritual lassitude, ennui, boredom, dissatisfaction, and restlessness.

8 This prayer (*Deus qui omni cor*) was one of the introductory prayers said by the celebrant of the Mass in the uniquely English Medieval Sarum Ordinary (and thus not to be found in the Roman Missal). An earlier English-language version of this prayer stands at the beginning of the great anonymous 13th-century English spiritual text, *The Cloud of Unknowing*: "GOD, unto whom all hearts be open, and unto whom all will speaketh, and unto whom no privy thing is hid, I beseech Thee so for to cleanse the intent of mine heart with the unspeakable gift of Thy grace, that I may perfectly love Thee, and worthily praise Thee. Amen." Its inclusion in the *Cloud* text indicates its private use by contemplatives.

That all the disorder and deformity of nature depicted in Cole's scene, as well as the demonic figures plaguing his journey, mirror the Soul's inner state—his thoughts, if you will—is explained explicitly by Cole (or, in the poem, this is explained *to* Cole by his guiding soul):

> This is the crisis—this the decisive hour
> In life's swift fever—balance Life and Death.
> *Adversity's* cold storm and *Sorrow's* power
> *Temptation* desperate with changeful breath
> Break with unmitigated fury on the Man,
> And Pleasure once so fair is sicklied o'er and wan.
>
> And earthly hopes are wrecked and cherished joy;
> And *friends estranged*; or turned to foes; or gone
> *Youth's crown of Glory faded and for aye:*[9]
> O'er Earth o'er Heaven a dusky pall is thrown:
> Affection's treasured things are found to fly
> Sink in the silent tomb, or vanish witheringly.
>
> Young Love's delicious river soon ran dry
> And wasted in life's wilderness of drought;
> *Ambition that once filled the ample sky*
> *Was but a dazzling cloud with tempest fraught:*[10]
> All, perished in the World or lost in Death
> As wastes in frosty air the warm and vaporous breath.
>
> The *heart*[11] doth suffer violence, racked and riven
> By the earthly blasts of earthly ill.
> *Burthened with sin* all vainly hath it striven
> Like a huge oak upon a wind-swept hill
> As tortured branches lash the Autumnal gale[12]
> And struggling yield their umbrage with a lengthened wail . . .[13]

Cole tells us nothing specific about the Soul's alleged "burthen" of "sin."

9 Recall that the youth in the previous scene was chasing after "The tempting semblance of a conqueror's crown / And wreath to bind the brows of him who wins renown."

10 In other words, the beguiling vision in the "Youth" scene has turned out to be the tempest of this scene. The "dazzling cloud" has become the dismal demonic cloud above the rapids.

11 The inner person. We are here clued in to the fact that what we see in this scene is an allegory of the Soul's interior condition.

12 The wind-blasted trees in the painting thus correspond in this reading to "the heart" of the voyager.

13 Tymn, *Thomas Cole's Poetry*, 155–56. Emphases added.

For that matter, he details nothing about the "Adversity," "Sorrow," and "Temptation" that plagues him, or how his friends might have become estranged. Cole speaks in generalities because this central figure — even if Cole conceived him as somewhat autobiographical — is himself inclusive of everyone; he represents all of us as individuals, with our own "burthens" and histories. There are very few who could look at this scene (or the whole series) and fail to perceive something pertinent to themselves in it. The more the years of our lives accumulate, the more we recognize ourselves for who and what we are (this is part of that wisdom which life should teach us). Our regrets and insight into ourselves grow as we grow. Or, rather, they *should* grow. Our outward trials, big and small, are frequently the means for waking us up. We look back and see our foolishness for what it was, our bad choices, our petty cruelties to other persons and other creatures, our arrogance, our lust, and so on. If we have lived long enough, we see more and more in our past thoughts, words, and deeds that trouble us — though we should not be so troubled that we don't seek the grace to change in the present. If we are becoming more interiorly sensitive to the selves we have been and are, we are moving along the right track. We may even come close to despair, as the Soul in the painting appears to have done. Nevertheless, it is only through trials that we gain — or should gain — awareness and acuity as we age. Admittedly, many will not gain such interior clarity, at least not in this life. Be that as it may, the oft-cited ancient Greek aphorism, "know thyself," can apply to what the trials of the Soul are all about.[14]

Those who may justifiably balk at the idea that the trials Cole mentions (and others far worse that have been inflicted from outside by the powerful and violent on the innocent, the persecuted, the enslaved, and so on since time immemorial) are somehow the workings of providence for the sole purpose of our gaining wisdom and self-knowledge might instead try taking a somewhat more existential view here. That is to say, they might begin with what *is* rather than what they assume *should be* the case in life, putting the question of God

---

14 It is not only the Greeks who cherished this maxim. We find it in some form in all the wisdom traditions of humankind. One example is that found in the *Tao Te Ching* (Chapter 33):

> He who knows others is learned;
> He who knows himself is wise.
> He who conquers others has power of muscles;
> He who conquers himself is strong.

(Lin Yutang's translation)

and providence to one side for the moment. Empirically and pragmatically speaking, then, we could still say that what Cole depicts allegorically is true of our lives. We do have an inner moral compass (from whatever source); we have taken wrong turns and gone "off-course" (sinned, in other words) and know it; we have hurt others and ourselves in numerous ways; we do know the consequences in our lives of our past actions and words; we do harbor regrets, and so on—and all these things and their magnitude do become clearer to us if we are, in fact, maturing as human beings. We discover, if we are sound of mind, that we can no longer claim ignorance as our excuse, as we might have done in our younger years. We are, pleasant and unpleasant, for good and ill, getting to "know ourselves," especially if we engage in some practice of healthy introspection. We *should* be growing wiser with age, whether we view that growth as the work of providence (in this "vale of Soul-making" or "soul-development") or as a real psychological need in an unpredictable universe. Either way, it amounts to the same overall picture, and the question of God's envelopment of the whole remains an open consideration for us (however we might conceive of "God"). In other words, Cole's sacred vision remains allegorically true and intact, and it still has the power to resonate within us, even if we are uncomfortable with terms like "providence."

In the poem, Cole at first fears that nothing has the power to save the voyager from death. He receives a stern rebuke from his guide for harboring such a thought: "Doubter! Thou yet mayest find / That what appears the greatest evil brings / Supremest good . . ." He is reminded that "the Guardian Angel sitteth yet / Benignant 'mong the stormy clouds . . . She waits with joy the prayer which heavenward now / The Voyager uplifts . . ."[15] Again Cole protests that the terrors and trials seem to him extravagant—it is a "fearful-over-perilous way / To lead but [only] to yon Ocean's misty horror gray [which is to say, it leads only to death] . . ." Isn't this much too horrific a route to travel, in other words, which leads to the grave at the end? Cole wants an answer, like all of us. Why evil and why death? About the latter, he says:

> And must the Voyager, these perils past
> Dwell ever on that vast and gloomy main,
> And on its lethean[16] bosom dull be cast,

---

15 Tymn, *Thomas Cole's Poetry*, 155.

16 A reference to Lethe, the river of forgetfulness in Hades according to Greek and Roman mythology. Dante is dipped into it and drinks from it at the summit of Mount Purgatory, so

Dreamless, eternally to sleep? Then vain
Would seem his Birth, his Youth, his Manhood prime;
Strange, useless burthens on the drooping wings of Time.[17]

Remembering that Cole's "guide" is, in fact, Cole himself, we have here an interesting interior dialogue between doubt and faith taking place. A more jaded reader could perhaps regard this as just a poetic conceit. I tend to see it as sincere — that Cole really did wrestle with his doubts and fears and needed to hold before himself faith and hope. True skepticism (which means scrutiny, not rejection — it isn't merely reducible to "doubt") is not the enemy of faith so much as its refiner. So it is that Cole questions his own soul honestly, and his soul responds with what is, in fact, *self*-rebuke. Again, we see this inner doubleness reflected in the painting: there is the supplicating, terrified voyager helplessly cast on the frenzied rapids below, and there is also the shining, transcendent Angel above — and these two, I dare say, are one. Likewise with Cole and Cole's "soul" in the poem.

Cole is again met with reproof, preparing the way for the fourth and final scene of the series:

Yet! Yet distrustful and forgetful ever
Dull to *the voice of wisdom*! I have said,
Death's pallid hand the cloudy veil shall sever
And wonder Ocean widely, darkly spread,
Be as a curtain quickly drawn away
And open like the Morn for a surpassing day.[18]

Once again, we have a reference to *wisdom* — Cole is accused of being "ever dull" to its "voice." We should take note that this "voice of wisdom" dwells within him, despite his self-reproach and confessed "dullness" to it. It's a "still, small voice," growing within him. He isn't devoid of it. He has reason to trust what it says to him, assuming he listens. One is reminded of the words of Cole's contemporary, Emerson: "Trust thyself: every heart vibrates to that iron string."[19] For Emerson, this was nothing less than the voice of God speaking within us, and Cole's "soul" — his guide in the poem — is also nothing less

---

that his past sins may be forgotten before ascending into Paradise (*Purgatorio* XXXIII). Here, however, Cole is referring to death itself as the forgetting of everything in life. One's life and all its memories, he fears, is merely extinguished.

17 Ibid., 156–57.

18 Ibid., 157. Emphasis added.

19 Ralph Waldo Emerson, "Self-Reliance," in *Essays and Lectures* (New York: Library of America, 1983), para. 3.

than the voice of God. Likewise, the Angel whose radiance pierces through the darkness overshadowing the vessel is the messenger of God.

What we might take away from this, then, before moving on to the last scene is simply this: Cole in the poem is learning to trust the voice of wisdom within himself, and the Soul in the allegorical painting is learning to do the same in the midst of—and, as Cole would have us believe, largely because of—his trials and tribulations. And should this vision resonate with us who reflect on it, there's reason to think the same may be happening within us as well.

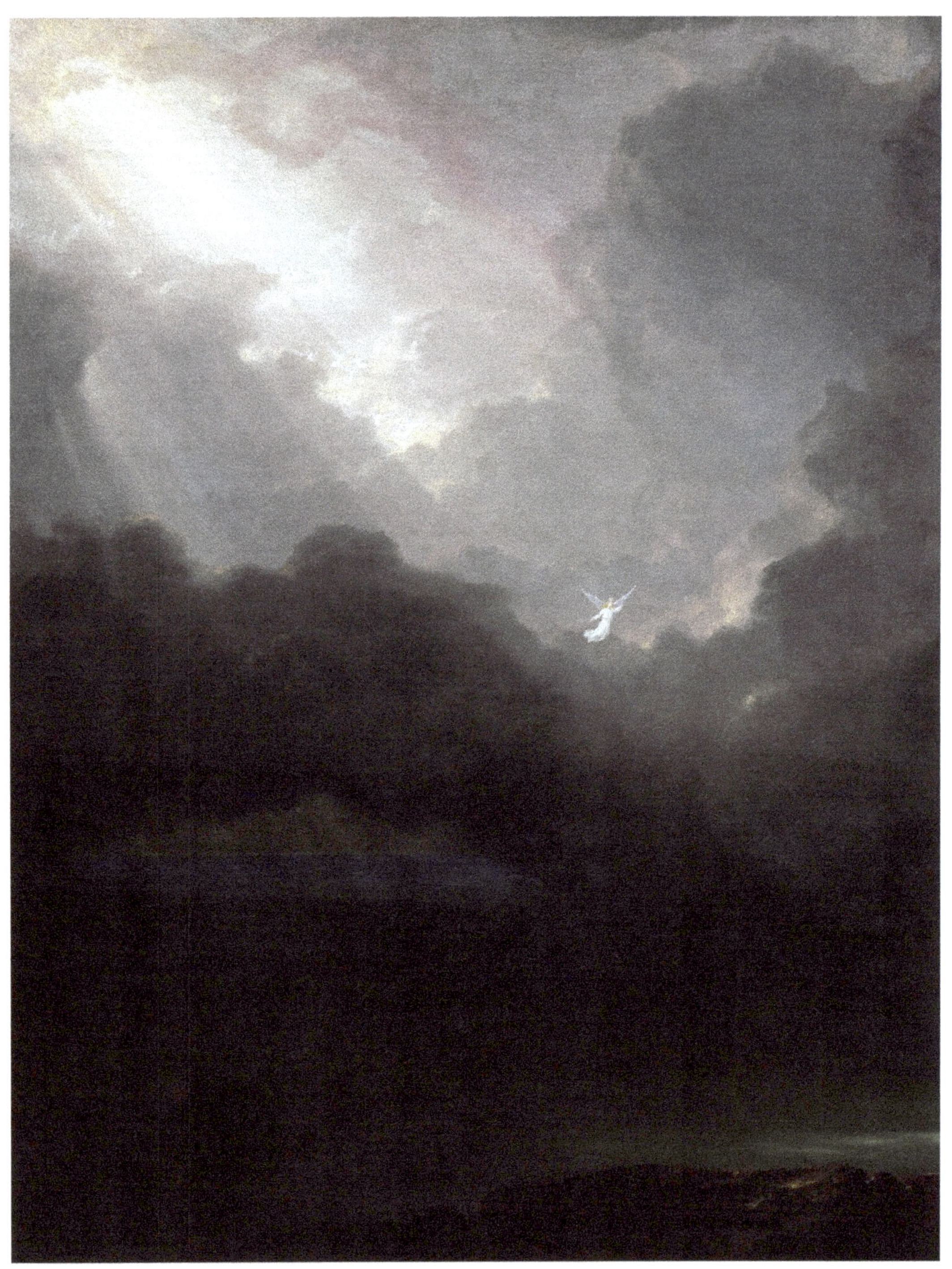

"OLD AGE," DETAIL

VI. "Old Age"

NOT ALL INTERpretations of *The Voyage of Life* have been consistent. No doubt, one reason for the few differing views advanced from time to time has been the difficulty of consulting Cole's interpretive poem. As of this date, it is not easily found online (at least, I haven't been able to track it down on the net), and there is only one edition of Cole's collected poems in print.[1] As examples of different explanations of *Voyage*, I can offer two—one recent and one nearly as old as the series itself. The first I came across while preparing to write this book. I found it (perhaps unsurprisingly) on a politically Libertarian website. The best aspect of this first example is that it does, in fact, make use of the poem, so its author must have had the latter at hand. However, it was this evident fact that made me wonder how he arrived at the interpretation he did. The author proposed that *Voyage* contains a message about the "national" situation in Cole's day, corresponding in some ways to his earlier series, *The Course of Empire*. According to this reading, the central figure—whom I have been referring to as the Soul—is an American "everyman," and the series is a call for individuals to struggle for what is right in a Jacksonian America headed in a dangerous direction—a danger epitomized by the election of James K. Polk in 1844 (the year in which, coincidentally enough, Cole wrote his explanatory poem). Cole feared that Polk's expansionist policies constituted a destructive force. Since this was Cole's political view, the series must, in turn, be an exhortation in art addressed to the sturdy American soul to be ready to resist strenuously—or so argues this purported explanation. Hence the poem's concluding lines: "He must

1 One can purchase a copy from the publisher here: https://www.shumwaypublisher.com/shop/item.aspx?itemid=28.

"OLD AGE," DETAIL

trust in God and strike, who conquers in the fight."[2] The "fight" is a political one.

I have no interest here in going into the history of the period or to argue at any length against the proposal that Cole's series is a veiled political message. Without assigning motives to the writer, it's fair to say simply that, for some, everything boils down to politics. But although Cole was politically aware and genuinely dismayed about the track upon which he saw the United States moving, there is no reason to read his political concerns into *The Voyage of Life*. There is no evidence, in other words, even considering the historical coincidence, for entertaining the idea. Cole's politics were one feature of his character, and so to that extent we might make a tenuous connection between it and *Voyage*. But this series has to do with the shaping of an individual's personal character in general, and not with any single feature that stems from that (such as one's political opinions). Still, this is an example of how far interpretive ingenuity can stretch Cole's straightforward allegory. Cole wrote, as we noted in the first chapter, that his aim was to make the series "perfectly intelligible." While an obscure parable about contemporary national issues might conceivably have been thought "intelligible" to some at the time, it's unlikely that he had any such private intention in mind, one he never even hinted at to anyone else. It's safe to say that *Voyage* had another, simpler purpose in view—one which Cole himself made explicit more than once.

If we can rule out a political interpretation, then, there is still another older one that comes much nearer to Cole's stated purpose. That said, I believe it errs by stressing too much the "spiritual" nature of the series' allegory. According to this other interpretation, the series is specifically about Christian conversion and initiation, and the "spiritual growth" that's expected to follow. The series begins, in this construal, with the central figure's *spiritual* infancy, then moves on to depict his youthful *spiritual* presumptuousness, proceeds to his consequential adult *spiritual* struggles, and ends with his ultimate *spiritual* repose. The figure's maturation from painting to painting is therefore that of a religious neophyte in the arduous process of growing into a proficient Christian disciple. Nor is this interpretation to be casually dismissed. No less than Cole's own friend, biographer, and priest, Louis Legrand Noble, suggested as much:

> Again to state a fact with respect to the series, *as applicable to the artist himself*: while the Voyage of Life [sic] is the expression of *his own full conviction of, and conversion to*, the truth of the gospel, this is the

2 Tymn, *Thomas Cole's Poetry*, 160.

> manifestation and memento of his regeneration or spiritual birth, and also of *his sanctification, renewal, or spiritual growth.*[3]

In short, Noble suggests that Cole was depicting his own personal "voyage" of discipleship from that of baptizand (an "infant Christian" of forty-one years) to the great destination of his becoming a ripe old Christian prepared to meet his Lord.

Noble is certainly not mistaken to apply to the series a decidedly Christian interpretation, and, after all, he knew Cole well and so he could advance his interpretation with credibility. To my mind, though, it appears that Noble was prone to interpret his deceased friend through the filter of his own beliefs (a characteristic we could all just as easily be guilty of with our friends). Put plainly, Cole's vision wasn't as narrow in perspective as Noble's interpretation indicates. It was not so "spiritual" in character as to be solely about Christian conversion and its aftermath—and much less, no matter how "autobiographical" in some sense it might have been, strictly about his personal "voyage of discipleship." Cole's was a broader vision, more fully "humanistic" in nature than Noble might have allowed, encompassing in its purview all aspects of human life. The voyage he depicts takes us from *physical*—not just "spiritual"—birth to natural death. What lies beyond is left in mystery, outside this world, although he indicates that his glimpse of its glory cannot be expressed in his poem. The humanism of Cole, the influence of which gives the series its most attractive quality, was indisputably *Christian* in character. But it was not a partial or sectarian Christianity which informed it. Given what he himself had to say about the series, Cole seems to have been taken with a vision of the *common* "voyage" of humanity, on which *every* human soul is embarked. He is not preoccupied with borders, national or spiritual. For Cole, there was no apparent inconsistency between the universal human experience and "the truth of the gospel" he embraced. The latter broadened his perspective; it didn't constrain it.

So, the series is neither a sort of visual American political tract nor a narrowly defined "spiritual" one. We are right to steer clear of both interpretations. Rather, what has Cole done? I believe, to put it simply, he has given us an iconography of lived experience, at once both fully human and richly spiritual in its dimensions (two aspects of human persons, whatever their backgrounds, that belong together). Behind these four paintings stand ages of Western and Christian thought regarding human existence and its meaning, depicted

---

3 Noble, *Life and Works*, 293. Emphasis added.

anew with the backdrop of a mythic version of the American landscape. If I were to presume to say what I see philosophically articulated by the imagery of the series, it might be something along the lines of Søren Kierkegaard's oft-quoted insight: "Philosophy is perfectly right in saying that life must be understood backwards. But then one forgets the other clause—that it must be lived forwards."[4] What Cole is doing is giving us both a picture of life as seen backwards from the perspective of its final scene, and simultaneously forward when viewed in sequence.

We will come back to this thought, but first let us look more closely at the final scene as Cole depicts it in order to see better how it might be said to apply.

The vessel has arrived at the ocean. It is midnight, the waters are still, and we can see the expanse stretching out before the Soul to the distant horizon. The dominant colors in the painting are charcoal, brown, grays, faded rose and gold where the light streams from on high, and the water about the boat is murky with somber shades of green. Cole stresses the gloomy nature of the scene in his poem:

> "Behold!" the voice then said: "The closing scene
> Of best humanity." The winds had ceased
> Their raving and the floods their roar—serene
> The air yet steeped in gloom as is the East
> When Earth's broad shadow o'er itself extends
> And far beneath the Main the evening sun descends.
>
> No hills of green, no gentle flowery vales
> No breezes fresh from out the crystal deeps
> No blithe birds warbling oft repeated tales;
> But silence, leaden silence, such as keeps
> The tongue fast bound the straining ear awakes
> As when the judge's sentence on the prisoner breaks.
>
> There flowed the river; but with sluggish pace
> And met and mingled with the Ocean dun...
> Still the eye caught the dim and shadowy shore,
> The last bare headlands of the dark terrene;
> Herbless, desolate, glimmering and obscure;

4 Howard V. Hong and Edna H. Hong, ed. and trans., *Søren Kierkegaard's Journals and Papers, Vol. 1, A–E* (Bloomington: Indiana University Press, 1967), *JP* I, 1030; *Pap.* IV A 164.

As landscape by the troubled dreamer seen,
Their shattered forms down sinking one by one
Into the deep of many deeps, the fathomless unknown.[5]

What Cole gives us in this description is an impression of death itself. In his grand metaphor, it is an immense ocean of stillness; it is dark, somber, a "fathomless unknown." It is, in other words, an alien environment, dead silent, devoid of familiar landscape and nature. It is entirely unlike the world the old Soul has left behind.

We can see that the boat in which he sits is shattered and slowly sinking; not only is its rudder long gone, but the sandglass (which signified the waning of time) that once adorned the prow has been broken off and is also lost. The sand has not only run out, but frame, glass, and all have disappeared forever. The boat itself has ceased to move as well. We might see this as indicating the cessation of the body's animation in death.

Broken that prow which once glanced o'er the stream;
Its Hours ensculptured all in gold were gone,
And gushed the floods through many a gaping seam:
It stopped—it settled—like a thing of stone:—
Some ponderous rock that 'cross the plain is sent;
Which labors on and on 'till with its labor spent.[6]

The aged Soul, bald and gray-bearded ("an ancient Man, / Withered and blighted by the frosts of time"[7]), looks away from us and up toward his Angel who is shown descending to receive him. There is an "upside-down" arc of clouds that appears to be the reverse of the arc of the cavern's entrance in the first scene, but this celestial entrance leads upwards into the heavens, not into the bowels of the earth from which the infant had emerged. Through the clouds come shafts of light, and one can discern, if one looks closely, at least eight more angels within the radiance (the imagery may remind the viewer of the "tunnel of light" recounted by those who have had near-death experiences). Cole notes that the Angel, hitherto unseen by the voyager, is now once more visible to him. This is, as Cole explains, because the Soul is leaving behind his earthly body.[8]

---

5 Tymn, *Thomas Cole's Poetry*, 157–58.

6 Ibid., 158.

7 Ibid.

8 "[F]lesh and blood cannot inherit the kingdom of God; neither doth corruption inherit incorruption." (1 Corinthians 15:50)

The Old man saw the Spirit for the earth
Was falling from his soul and from his eyes
The film of blinding clay as falls the swarth
Envelope from the opening bud. Surprise!
O blest! To see, undreaming, spirit forms
Immaculate and free from all that earth deforms.[9]

Cole concludes the poem rapturously, describing the divine vision as best he can, and—in a stanza reminiscent of both Dante and of John Henry Newman's poem, *The Dream of Gerontius* as well[10]—he averts his gaze from the blinding glory of God:

I turned mine eyes; I could no longer gaze
Upon the Splendour, which intenser grew
And live; To my relief a dimming haze
Dropt like a curtain dark and shut the view;
But 'neath the weight of Glory which had shown
Upon the Earth's low bosom prostrate I was thrown.[11]

---

9 Tymn, *Thomas Cole's Poetry*, 159. The word "earth" here, not being capitalized, means the metaphorical "earthly clay" from which we are made. Cole's dualism of body and soul/spirit is pronounced.

10 Newman was Cole's contemporary, born just twenty days after the latter. *The Dream of Gerontius* was written in 1865, twenty-one years after Cole's poem. In Newman's poem, when the departed "soul" is taken by his "angel" before God, and the former beholds the divine splendor, we have the following dialogue, in which the departed soul begs to be taken away to Purgatory and there become fit to enter into its presence forever:

SOUL
I go before my Judge. Ah!. . . .

ANGEL
. . . Praise to His Name!
The eager spirit has darted from my hold,
And, with the intemperate energy of love,
Flies to the dear feet of Emmanuel;
But, ere it reach them, the keen sanctity,
Which with its effluence, like a glory, clothes
And circles round the Crucified, has seized,
And scorch'd, and shrivell'd it; and now it lies
Passive and still before the awful Throne.
O happy, suffering soul! for it is safe,
Consumed, yet quicken'd, by the glance of God.

SOUL
Take me away, and in the lowest deep
There let me be,
And there in hope the lone night-watches keep,
Told out for me.
There, motionless and happy in my pain,
Lone, not forlorn,—
There will I sing my sad perpetual strain,
Until the morn.
There will I sing, and soothe my stricken breast,
Which ne'er can cease
To throb, and pine, and languish, till possest
Of its Sole Peace.
There will I sing my absent Lord and Love:—
Take me away,
That sooner I may rise, and go above,
And see Him in the truth of everlasting day.

11 Tymn, *Thomas Cole's Poetry*, 160.

At this point, there is nothing left for Cole except to provide the "moral" of the series (no doubt, these stanzas would have caused Robert Hughes to recoil, but—ah, well):

> There long I lay mingling my sighs and tears
> Recalling all the Vision to my mind,
> Its varied scenes, its many hopes and fears
> Its seasons four mysteriously combined,
> How through bright Childhood's vale the river flowed
> Youth, Manhood, Age, to reach the mighty flood.
>
> But my soul spoke and roused me—"Rise
> Dwell not inactive on the Vision true
> Remember that Life's River swiftly hies
> Toward the great Deep and thou hast much to do:
> The Vision teaches when divined aright
> That he must trust in God and strike, who conquers in the fight."[12]

As with Cole in these last lines, then, so with us who look at his work. We take it in whole ("recalling all the Vision" and remembering "that Life's River swiftly hies / Toward the great Deep") and allow "the Vision true" to sink in.

The last line, in my opinion, is clumsy. Throughout the series and poem, the allegory's guiding image has been a voyage, not a fight. To bring in the language of battle here at the poem's conclusion ("strike," "conquers") doesn't fit the overall context and seems more like an intrusion than a logical summing up. Still, this is Cole's poem and Cole's conclusion, and so we should try to understand its meaning rather than carp about its suitability. Of one thing we can be certain: Cole's final words have nothing to do with national politics. Rather, if a "fight" fits in anywhere in the course of this voyage, it can only be a fight within the voyager's self. The final exhortation is best read, then, as "trust God and don't despair." In other words, the moral to all of us is this: you have seen the big picture that the series illustrates, you have seen that trials are unavoidable, that you will make poor decisions in life, you will struggle, even struggle with your faith and your confidence, you will know fear and uncertainty, you will have many things to regret, you will encounter death and sorrow and loss, and you will reach the conclusion of your life. Realize all this, remember it, and know that through it all you will overcome, one way or the other. What is it, then, that should be *done* considering all the above? It

12 Ibid.

is to keep your eyes set on the goal, which—as we saw when discussing the "Youth" above—is to grow in wisdom; "fight" to gain it. And the real "fight" will take place within you.

Cole died of pleurisy in 1848, just ten days after his forty-seventh birthday. He never made it to the old age he depicted in the final scene. And yet, one has the feeling that he comprehended very well what it meant—to return to Kierkegaard's terminology—to understand life "backwards," from the point of view of someone near to life's end. What Cole did not reach in literal years he appears to have reached by way of his spiritual imagination. I have little doubt that he saw himself in the final scene, just as he had seen himself in the three that preceded it. He was able to see and "feel" himself as someone old and dying. And, in effect, Cole is urging us to do the same as we contemplate the series. Remember, the series is—in great part—a *memento mori*. Throughout the course of its images, it has reminded us repeatedly of the inevitability of death—not just death as a generality, but our personal deaths. Once again, if the infant's outstretched arms are not only extended in joy but also as a foreshadowing of crucifixion and hence mortality, and if the youth's distracted gaze fails to see the winding river's deadly rapids ahead, and if the grown man's posture resembles that of Christ in agony in Gethsemane, fearful of suffering and death, then that stark reminder is there for us in every scene.

Accordingly, the final scene is more than just the *destination* at the end of the trip. It is *the proper standpoint* from which we observe all the scenes preceding it. Up to this stage, the Soul has been voyaging and living his life "forwards," although in the first three scenes he could not see coming what we, the viewers, could see. The infant was innocent and clueless; the voyage was all still ahead of him and well beyond his comprehension. The destination was nowhere in sight. The youth was ignorant, but self-confident and ambitious, oblivious to the dangers he yet had to face. He knew, as an educated ignoramus, that death was out there, far ahead, but it was nothing for him to dwell on morbidly with such an unshakable future still ahead and, he thought, in view. The grown man, however, was swept up in a destructive tempest, unable to navigate or foresee the outcome of his journey. Death as a threat had now unsettled him to the core of his being—he might not survive; he could be dashed on the rocks and go under. All the while, viewers who can see the entire series stretched out before them know very well what is coming in due course: that the river will finally bring the irreparably damaged bark down to the dark midnight sea, where death awaits the Soul, and that it is from that final vantage point only that all the preceding scenes will find their largest perspective. Cole, it is important to note, has already preceded us there, looking at the sequence "backwards." That last scene is where he stands, surveying the full length of the river, the full length of the Soul's life. His poem presents himself as moving "forward" scene by scene, his own "soul" as his guide explaining each consecutive picture to him as he proceeds, but we know very well that he's written that poem from the outset with the end in plain view.

From the end, then, we too stand in a position to look backwards and—using Kierkegaard's word—"understand," if only partially (which is all we can ever do), the twists and turns of the entire voyage and how they led to this final, liminal moment. It's not just Cole's voyage or the figurative Soul's voyage; we "get it"—this has been *our* voyage, too, and likewise in this final scene we see "our" death. Even the wrong turn, the failed attempt to reach one's own dream (the vision of the city in the clouds), the tragedies and trials of what ensued (the tempest, rocks, and rapids)—even these potential dead-ends and apparent disasters—turned out not to be *wrong* in any ultimate sense. The same is true in our lives. If providence means anything at all, it means that whatever direction we go as we move forward, a wrong choice or development can present us with the possibility of making a right one later. We are always in the long process of self-correcting, self-righting, and soul-development. Through the perseverance of the Soul—not without his desperate prayers, tears, and struggling faith—all his ills are met by a providence that has been at work transforming him for the best throughout the journey. At the end, he is old and weary, surely, but he is also ready to move into that next, incomprehensible stage of his existence. Again, we, like him in the allegory, see the journey in perspective *because we see it whole*. We see it backwards.

The Voyage of Life moves us to realize two important things in this regard. First, the series says to us that the only reliable perspective in life comes by way of experience, and experience comes with age—and in an impatient world, that may sound discouraging. But, discouraging or not, it is how life—ineluctably lived forward—actually is. We may as well accept it and see in it the opportunity it presents. Time is the key factor. Our earlier perspectives in life were bound to be misconceived, and many of our earlier ideas and beliefs had to undergo metamorphosis as we matured. Life saw to that. It is the elderly and experienced who can — or, at any rate, *should* — look back on the lives they have lived with some acquired understanding.

This vision seems almost inconceivable (possibly even something to deride) in our culture. But our culture, such as it is, is an anomaly in human history. Most traditional cultures have placed a high premium on age, and it is usually expected that the elders in a community should have acquired a measure of wisdom. Of course, we also know that many elders are not wise and that many others never even become elders. But Cole is presenting an allegory of the universal standard of growth in maturity, and we should regard the series in that light. Without doubt, there are exceptions to the standard, but this series is about the standard and not the exceptions. Again, we should remember that he himself was an exception, dying before reaching old age. Nonetheless, this is in some crucial ways an older person's series of paintings, despite that. And even though I began this book by stating the impact it had on me as a child, in my later years — at this writing I am nearly two decades older than was Cole at his death — I recognize it as a work born of lived experience and its resulting insight.

And so, the second thing Cole leads us to realize is that we can, *at any age*, begin to contemplate the whole sequence of human life. We can situate ourselves imaginatively alongside the Soul in his old age — as Cole evidently did — and see the bigger picture *as if* we were looking "backwards," just as he does. And we can, as I said, do that at any age. We can imaginatively "look back" at our own lives; it is a meditative perspective we can adopt. It can become a practice, and through that practice we can thereby plant some seeds of wisdom within ourselves.

Again, wisdom primarily means to "know ourselves," and this in turn means — in a sense — looking at our lives "backwards" even while we are living it "forwards." Instead of wishing to stay young, which is futile and foolish anyway, we need to accept age and finally death as inevitable, teaching ourselves to keep these before our eyes all along the way. They are the destination of each of our own earthly voyages of life. If we can learn the practice, at whatever stage we have reached, of standing back and imaginatively surveying our lives "backwards," from the vantage point of the elder we are destined to become, we might find ourselves gaining richer understanding than we ever thought possible. The better we know ourselves, where we have been and where we are headed, recognizing as well that we have made poor decisions and yet survived and kept moving despite ourselves, the better we should understand, accept, and have sympathy for others as well. Cole, I believe, lived at a time when such reflection was more commonly practiced, even among the young—so common, in fact, that it didn't require much comment. We would do well to relearn how to reflect on such things, assaying our thoughts, words, and deeds in light of our end.

In conclusion, Thomas Cole has left us a remarkable allegory in four intelligible scenes about life and life's purpose: the development of our souls and growth in wisdom during the few short decades we have been allotted. We may find it useful, like a good map, as we pilot our individual vessels along the river of time down to the midnight sea.

The Voyage of Life

I. PART ONE

Forth through the ancient shadowy woods as one
Who hath no being but his thought I wended
Instinctively. The deep and solemn tone,
The holy gloom harmoniously blended
With musings grave and fond of Life and Death
And Immortality; which waits our parting breath.

I dreamed not; but before me rose a wall
Of rock stupendous: crag on crag was piled
In a gray mountainous heap and over all
The towering ramparts shadows fell from wild
Portentous clouds that ever restlessly
Hid the far summits from the wondering eye.

And in the bosom of that stoney pile
Which seemed the ruin of a shattered world
Heaped skyward by some Titan's mighty toil
A cavern yawned like death and changeful curled
Across its sombre arches vast and wide
Pale spectral mists; as though its awful depths to hide.

But yet the eye unwilling to be barred
Pierced far within the antre's silent womb,
Arch beyond arch with many a fissure scarred,
Perceived, until impenetrable gloom
Sealed unto human vision, human thought
The secret things with which its depths were fraught.

From the mysterious bosom of that cave
A gentle river took its winding way,
Reflecting freshly in the crystal wave
Rocks, sky and herbage which the glancing ray
Of the uprising sun made rosy light:
A wreath of glory on the dewy verge of night.

Murmuring it left the dim and shadowy gloom
And joyous as a thing of life it flowed
Where flowers in fragrant companies did bloom
Bespangled all with dew and sweetly bowed
Their beauteous faces o'er the placid stream,
Narcissus-like involved in love's delusive dream.

The song of birds uprose on every side
And mingled sweetly in the jocund air
That frolicked free across the dimpling tide
And o'er that paradise of flowers so fair;
And it did seem as though the sky and earth
Sang choral hymns at some blessed Angel's birth.

Gliding out from the deep recess there came
A wondrous Vessel, golden was its bow,
Which flashed across the waters like a flame.
Of wingèd Hours the Bark was wrought—The prow
A laughing form with such like intertwined;
But dark confused and crowded were the shapes behind.

It bore two beings; one an infant child
That laughed and sported on a flowery bed;
The other was a form of aspect mild;
Radiant it stood and o'er its glorious head
A star hung tremulous and brighter did appear
Than Venus when the morn from cloud and mist is clear.

Its azure wings were poised in buoyant rest
As though just ceased from fanning heavenly air;
One hand the Vessel's rudder graceful pressed,
The other stretched with most benignant care
O'er the child. It was a beauteous form and face
Such like doth meet at Heaven's Gate the soul that findeth grace.

"What meaneth this," with earnest voice I cried,
"The landscape bright, the river's flow serene,
And those two Voyagers—" My soul replied:
"Life hath her pictures of each varied scene
The mortal pilgrim sees, wrought on the heart
In colors clear and strong that never can depart.

"Experience is the artist and she toils
Incessantly with ever painful care;
Whether beneath the sun the landscape smiles
Or storms obscure; the lights and shades are there;
But Reason, Passion, Prejudice and Time
Do give the after-tone discordant or sublime.

"By thee now standing midway on the height
Of contemplation not alone are seen
Pictures of the departing past; but sight
Of future scenes is opened through a screen
Of darkling clouds and mists fantastic lies
Across the tearful vision of thy longing eyes.

"By mortal man that River of dark source
Is named the 'Stream of Life'; with constant flow
With many a winding on its downward course,
At times it lags along with motion slow,
At times impetuous o'er the rocky steep
It journeyeth onward toward The Eternal Deep.

"There in that vast Profound—that darkest Dread
That Silence—that immeasurable Gloom,
The Breathless—Shoreless—the Un-islanded
Of the great World—of mighty Time the Tomb
It sinks, it vanishes and mortal eye
Perplexed and troubled, trembling turns on high.

"But human thought, thanks be to God, can soar
Triumphant on the wings of light divine
And take its flight above the Shadow hoar;
Where Angels in a land of beauty shine
In living light which is the Light of Light,
The everlasting day, that suffereth not the night.

"Thou wert such infant Voyager, all men
Have been—the thousands yet unborn will be
Cast in such mould and of such origin
Mysterious to themselves and even he
Who bore our sorrows; for us shed his blood
Was launched in that strange Bark and sailed the mystic flood.

"Know! innocence enshrines the infant-heart
Its tears are but as dew drops freshening joy;
For withering sin, as yet, can claim no part
Nor pale remorse bedim the beaming eye.
Children are buds of Heaven 'tis earthly air
That breeds the cankers, guilt and deadening despair.

"They have their Angels. Yonder dazzling shape
That steers the richly freighted bark is one
Of those who 'minister' and constant keep
A watch around us, leave us not alone
From infancy to age, whether is clear the sky;
Or robed in thunder-clouds dark demons hover high.

"We see them not with our dull mortal eyes,
Yet as Zephyr bears the thistle's down;
Or summer clouds in the cerulean skies,
About us their immaculate arms are thrown,
And nought but Giant Sin can drag us thence
Who grows and conquers by our disobedience."

"O Soul!" I cried! "Why linger not the Hours
In that blest clime of innocence? Why flowed
The stream so swiftly through the land of flowers?
Why did we leave Life's highest hill that glowed
'Mid light celestial? Where the breezes blow
Direct from Heaven, and seek these darker vales below?"

"A higher destiny is thine," replied
My soul "through trial, sorrow, darkness, pain
The road to far sublimer joys does lead
And lasting bliss by suffering we gain
And by the gloomy vale through which we tread
We reach the bliss that makes all earthly joy seem dead."

2. PART TWO

As the broad mountain where the shadows flit
Of clouds dispersing in the summer-breeze;
Or like the eye of one who high does sit
On Taormina's antique height and sees
The fiery Mount afar, the Ruin near at hand,
The flowers, the purple waves that wash the golden strand.

So changed my thought from light to shade;
At times exulting in the glow of hope, at times
In darkness cast by what my soul had said;
'Till sunk in reverie her words seemed chimes
From some far tower, that tell of mystial joy,
Or knell that fills the air as with a lingering sigh.

Again I raised my downcast eyes to look
Upon the scene so beautiful when lo!
The stream no longer from the cavern took
Its gentle way 'tween flowery banks and low
But through a landscape varied, rich and vast
Beneath a sky that dusky cloud had surely never passed.

Wide was the river; with majestic flow
And pomp and power it swept the curving banks
Like some great conqueror whose march is slow
Through tributary lands; while the abasèd ranks,
Shrinking give back on either hand o'erawed
As though they trembling felt the presence of a God.

And like some Wizard's mirror, that displays
The Macrocosm, it did reflect the sky,
Rocks, lawns and mountains with their purple haze,
And living things, the filmy butterfly,
The trembling fawn that drinks, the fluttering dove
And the triumphant eagle soaring far above.

And trees like those which spread their pleasant shade
O'er the green slopes of Eden, and the bowers
Of the once sinless pair, soft, intermingling made
Stood on each shore with branches lifted high
And caught eolian strains that wandered from the sky.

Far, far away the shining river sped
Toward the etherial mountains which did close
Fold beyond fold until they vanished
In the horizon's silver, whence uprose
A structure strangely beautiful and vast
Which every earthly fane Egyptian, Gothic, Greek, surpassed.

It seemed a gorgeous palace in the sky
Such as the glad sun builds above the deep
On summer-eve and lighteth dazzlingly,
Where towering clouds climb up the azure steep
And pinnacles on pinnacles fantastic rise
And ever-changing charm the wondering eyes.

There, rank o'er rank that climbed the crystal air
In horizontal majesty, were crossed
The multitudinous shafts, or ranged afar
Till in the blue perspective they were lost,
And arches linked with arches stretched along
Like to the mystic measures of an antique song.

An antique song whose half-discovered sense
Seems to spring forth from depths, as yet, unknown
And fills the heart with wonder and suspense
Until to thrilling rapture it is grown;
Breathless we listen to each wandering strain
And when the numbers cease, we listen still again.

Above the columned pile sublimely rose
A Dome stupendous; like the moon it shone
When first upon the orient sky she glows
And moves along the Ocean's verge alone;
And yet beyond, above, another sphere
And yet another, vaster, dimly did appear.

As though the blue supernal space were filled
With towers and temples, which the eye intent
Piercing the filmy atmosphere that veiled,
From glorious dome to dome rejoicing went,
And the deep folds of ether were unfurled
To show the splendors of a higher world.

But from the vision of the upper air
My eye descended to the lucid stream;
The wingèd Boat — the Voyagers were there;
But the fair Infant of my earlier dream
Now stood a Youth on manhood's verge, his eye
Flashing with confidence and hot expectancy.

Was lifted toward the sky-encastled scene,
His hand had grasped the helm once gently held
By that Angelic figure so serene,
And eager stretching toward the scene beheld,
His bosom heaved as if with secret powers
Possessed to tread the deep — to outstrip the flying Hours.

With face benignant yet impinged with sorrow,
As oft the sky of eve by melancholy cloud
Which though it doth forbode a stormy morrow
Is not less beautiful, the Angel stood
Upon the bank as from the Boat just freed
And waved her graceful hand and bade the Youth "God Speed."

As one emerging from some misty vale
Meets the glad splendor of the rising sun;
Or mariner who the wintry sea doth sail
Through opening wrack beholds the harbor won,
So did I gaze upon the charming scene
And in my joy forgot the vision Infantine.

When thus the Voice in plantive accents mild:
"Ah simple mortal Earth has many a show
That passes quickly — thou a credulous child,
All men are children and they thoughtless go
Through life's strange vale lingering by every flower
Forgetful life is labor and its term an hour.

"The scene before thee beautiful and bright
Is but a phantasm of Youth's heated brain
And doomed to fade as day before the night;
Fleeting its glory, transitory, vain;
Save that it teaches the meek humble soul
Earth's grandeur ne'er should be the spirit's Goal.

"Not that the earth foundationless is laid,
An unsubstantial thing, a cloud, a mist;
But 'tis a darkling soil wherein the seed
Of Virtue planted, tended may subsist
And washed by many tears may grow
To more enduring beauty than these gauds below.

"But mark the Youth, how filled his eager eye
With the bright exaltation.—See! he aims
To reach the portal of the palace high
Above whose cloudy arch resplendant flames
The tempting semblance of a conqueror's crown
And wreath to bind the brows of him who wins renown.

"And while he gazes greater glories rise
Higher yet higher; ardent young desire
With telescopic vision fills the skies.
Gay are the banks in verdurous attire
And swift the river floweth toward his hope
The palace stands beyond, reached by a gentle slope.

"Weak and deluded one! Dost thou not know
Thy Bark is hasting down the Stream of Life
And tarries not for any golden show
In pleasure's gardens though with beauty rife!
So doth the comet pass the planets by
Nor rests; but speeds on its appointed destiny.

"Does not thine eye perceive that when yon towers
Are well nigh gained with sudden sweep the stream,
And growing swiftness, shoots away and pours
Impetuous, towards a shadowy ravine deep
Cleft in the mountain's vast and misty side
As though it eager sought its thwarted floods to hide."

The voice had paused: "And is it thus" I cried,
"That Youth's fond hopes must ever pass away;
As empty dreams, untouched unsatisfied:
Why leaves the Angel on his dangerous way
The Voyager? That hand divine could steer
The willing Boat to where yon glittering domes uprear.

"And lingering by these fresh and verdant shores
E'en youth might live a long long life of joy
And shun perchance the torrent where it pours
Adown yon dread descent." To which reply
Came quickly, "Shrouded as now thou art in earth
Thou canst not see the end for which came mortal birth.

"In the Almighty mind the secret cause is laid;
This must thou learn, that our brief mortal life
Nor rests nor lingers; nor is checked nor stayed
By human skill or might howe'er so rife;
Nor is it in an Angel's godlike power
To lengthen out its wasting thread one single hour.

"Through feeble Infancy is steered the Bark of Life
By Angel hands; but growing man demands
The helm in confidence and dares the strife
Of the far-sweeping waves. The lurking sands,
The rapids foaming through the channel dim,
The roaring cataract are all unknown to him.

"Wisdom is born of sorrow and of care
And from man's conflicts with the world arise
A sense of weakness and of chilling fear
And driven from earth his hopes ascend the skies.
Thus is he launched upon the stream alone
To chasten pride and give young desire a holier tone.

"He is alone; but still deserted never
The Angel yet shall watch his perilous way;
And though the clouds of earth may seem to sever,
Still through the darkness shines the Angelic ray;
And in the hour of midnight o'er the deep
The Guardian Spirit kind will constant vigil keep."

3. PART THREE

Those closing accents fell upon my ear
Sweetly as dew upon the drooping flower
For in my thoughts were knit suspense and fear
Which grew to hope transmuted by their power,
So the first breeze of Spring upon the hills
With sighs awakes the buds and frees the ice-bound rills.

In gentle reverie my mind reposed
When lo! The vision changed—A dismal vale—
Its sides down stooping into night were bossed
With jagged rocks—above huge crags rose pale
And quivering in thick turbulent air
Like hell-affrighted spectres starting from their lair.

It seemed the Earthquake there had oped his jaws
And fierce Convulsion rent the ribs of Earth;
Darkness and light forgot their ancient laws.
It was a den where demons had their birth
Where voices strange and many a dusky form
Smote the strained ear and did the sky deform.

And down this valley's gulphy depths profound;
Where resting place is none; nor green retreat;
Where fear and death forever hover round,
On every blast their restless pinions beat;
The river of my Vision took its way
And left far, far behind the golden light of day.

Onward it dashed and with a tyrannic force
Swept o'er the fractured rocks and foamed and fell
And reeled from side to side with thunders hoarse:
Though broken off and baffled naught could quell:—
Athwart the steep the streaming floods did pour
And rocky fragments fell, dislodged amid the roar.

On a swift curve, a verge of glossy green,
Such Niagaras where its waters leap
The dizzy precipice, the Boat was seen
Fleet as a meteor thwart the midnight deep.
Like famished wolves when the scared prey is nigh,
The pale demoniac floods roared louder as for joy.

No more youth's sunshine like a halo spread
Around the Voyager's high imperial brow;
But Care's wan shadow settled on his head
As clouds their gloom upon the mountain throw.
His now the middle age when human thought
Ascends her highest tower with rich experience fraught.

So have we seen in some dense city's way
A frantic steed dash through the affrighted crowd
With his pale rider — to and fro they sway
With headlong speed mid shrieks and clamor loud
'Till by a sudden plunge he disappears. —
In dumb suspense we stand and quake with horrid fears.

"What now can save?" I cried. O ever blind
But to the present and the mask of things
Was quick replied: "Doubter! Thou yet mayest find
That what appears the greatest evil brings
Supremest good as blackest storms and rain
Bring freshness, beauty, glory in their passing train.

"Behold the Guardian Angel sitteth yet
Benignant 'mong the stormy clouds aloft
Kindling their blackness; like a Glory set
By God in midnight space — A sun whose soft
Unbroken light illumes some lonely sphere
That travelleth through depths of trackless ether drear.

"She waits with joy the prayer which heavenward now
The Voyager uplifts — Faith's earnest cry:
For rescued by that act the floods below
With all their fury; nor the tempest nigh;
Nor ocean, seen afar have power to harm;
Nor yet yon Demon Shapes terrific cause alarm.

"This is the crisis — this the decisive hour
In life's swift fever — balance Life and Death.
Adversity's cold storm and Sorrow's power
Temptation desperate with changeful breath
Break with unmitigated fury on the Man,
And Pleasure once so fair is sicklied o'er and wan.

"And earthly hopes are wrecked and cherished joy;
And friends estranged; or turned to foes; or gone
Youth's crown of Glory faded and for aye:
O'er Earth o'er Heaven a dusky pall is thrown:
Affection's treasured things are found to fly
Sink in the silent tomb, or vanish witheringly.

"Young Love's delicious river soon ran dry
And wasted in life's wilderness of drought;
Ambition that once filled the ample sky
Was but a dazzling cloud with tempest fraught:
All, perished in the World or lost in Death
As wastes in frosty air the warm and vaporous breath.

"The heart doth suffer violence, racked and riven
By the relentless blasts of earthly ill.
Burthened with sin all vainly hath it striven
Like a huge oak upon a wind-swept hill
As tortured branches lash the Autumnal gale
And struggling yield their umbrage with a lengthened wail.

"But as the Spring, the gentle Spring, draws nigh
To warm its mighty heart and swell its buds
To lift its fragrance and to beautify;
So through the Voyager's breast, amid these floods,
A living warmth shall steal and prayer shall rise
And yon attendant Spirit waft it to the skies.

"The Guardian watches yet the weltering bark
O'er the vexed floods adown the dizzy steep
Through rock-ribbed channels hideous and dark
Safely to guide him toward yon Ocean deep
Whose darkly boundless waves eternal silence keep."

My Teacher! Guide! Thou who hast kindly read
The meaning of these wondrous scenes to me
Still my heart trembles, like a fragile reed
By the lone shore where stamps the angry sea,
This is a fearful-over-perilous way
To lead but to yon Ocean's misty horror gray.

And must the Voyager, these perils past
Dwell ever on that vast and gloomy main,
And on its lethean bosom dull be cast,
Dreamless, eternally to sleep? Then vain
Would seem his Birth, his Youth, his Manhood prime;
Strange, useless burthens on the drooping Wings of Time.

"Yet! Yet distrustful and forgetful ever
Dull to the voice of wisdom! I have said,
Death's pallid hand the cloudy veil shall sever
And wonder Ocean widely, darkly spread,
Be as a curtain quickly drawn away
And open like the Morn for a surpassing day."

4. PART FOUR

Struck by my Mentor's serious reply
In sorrow I had clasped my hoods across
My tearful eyes; yet were my tears half joy;
For the quick sentence of rebuke did close
With breath of kindling hope and promise bright;
As broke upon the blind by Siloam's pool of light.

"Behold!" the voice then said: "The closing scene
Of best humanity." The winds had ceased
Their raving and the floods their roar—serene
The air yet steeped in gloom as is the East
When Earth's broad shadow o'er itself extends
And far beneath the Main the evening sun descends.

No hills of green, no gentle flowery vales
No breezes fresh from out the crystal deeps
No blithe birds warbling oft repeated tales;
But silence, leaden silence, such as keeps
The tongue fast bound the straining ear awakes
As when the judge's sentence on the prisoner breaks.

There, flowed the river; but with sluggish pace
And met and mingled with the Ocean dun
No more exulting in the headlong race;
But fainting as its destined Goal was won—
Last 'mid the boundless, as the single voice
When crowded multitudes do suffer; or rejoice.

Still the eye caught the dim and shadowy shore,
The last bare headlands of the dark terrene;
Herbless, desolate, glimmering and obscure;
As landscape by the troubled dreamer seen,
Their shattered forms down sinking one by one
Into the deep of many deeps, the fathomless unknown.

Oppressed I gazed: my thick and struggling sighs
Or checked by the silence would have filled the air;
But soon the winged Boat my eager eyes
Discerned—the Man—the Tempest-tossed was there.
O'er the unrippled flood with motion slow
As heavy laden, sinking—sinking moved the prow.

Broken that prow which once glanced o'er the stream;
Its Hours ensculptured all in gold were gone,
And gushed the floods through many a gaping seam:
It stopped,—it settled—like a thing of stone:—
Some ponderous rock that 'cross the plain is sent;
Which labors on and on 'till with its labor spent.

There sat the Voyager, an ancient Man,
Withered and blighted by the frosts of time:
Furrowed his cheek, his forehead bare and wan
As though the tempests of each earthly clime
Had broken o'er him in their fiercest mood
And he with patient soul their fury had withstood.

Then as the fulgent moon o'er ocean comes,
Spreading her wings of light at eventide,
I saw the Guardian's radiant flames
Hush the black midnight wave and swiftly glide
Through the illumined, fast dissolving wrack
And by the Voyager her airy station take.

The Old man saw the Spirit for the earth
Was falling from his soul and from his eyes
The film of blinding clay as falls the swarth
Envelope from the opening bud. Surprise!
O blest! To see, undreaming, spirit forms
Immaculate and free from all that earth deforms.

He saw the blessed Guardian of his way
And knew "his Angel"; ne'er before discerned;
And love and new-born joy broke in like day
Upon his heaven-illumined soul. He turned
To gaze upon the beauteous one, when lo!
As from the clouds strange music 'gan to flow.

Music it was, if thus is named in heaven
Those mingled gushes of Seraphic bliss
Which flowed like sunlight of the Spring-tide given
In beamy gold to wake the wilderness;
Or like the hymning of some circling band
Of joyous stars just sped from their Creator's hand.

Gently swelling, gently falling
Softer, sweeter yet it grows;
As when Summer's breeze is calling
Fragrance from the dewy rose.
Yes far sweeter and more thrilling
Were the soulèd sounds that fell,
All the airy concave filling
And the heart's most secret cell.
Tuneful breathings — voicèd hymning
Joined with harps of golden sound
Fill the spherèd concave brimming —
Shed rich harmony around.
Now the Trumpet's crystal voice
Lifteth up its notes of joy
Calling to the saved "Rejoice!
Enter through Heaven's portal high."
Back the murky clouds are driven
As the blackness of the sky
By the morning sun is riven

Angels! Angels! Blessed creatures!
Toward the Voyager descend;
Turn on him their holy features
Lit by joy that ne'er can end;
Down the streamy light they sweep
Round him wave their dazzling wings;
Lift him gently from the deep
Whisper to him wondrous things.
Swift he rises — Earth has left him
With its painful load of clay; —
Death or grief and sin hath reft him
And he soars — away! — away!

I turned mine eyes; I could no longer gaze
Upon the Splendour, which intenser grew
And live; To my relief a dimming haze
Dropt like a curtain dark and shut the view;
But 'neath the weight of Glory which had shone
Upon the Earth's low bosom prostrate I was thrown.

There long I lay mingling my sighs and tears
Recalling all the Vision to my mind,
Its varied scenes, its many hopes and fears
Its seasons four mysteriously combined,
How through bright Childhood's vale the river flowed
Youth, Manhood, Age, to reach the mighty flood.

But my soul spoke and roused me — "Rise
Dwell not inactive on the Vision true
Remember that Life's River swiftly hies
Toward the great Deep and thou hast much to do:
The Vision teaches when divined aright
That he must trust in God and strike, who conquers in the fight."

Catskill June 14, 1844

WORKS CITED AND CONSULTED

Martin Buber. *I and Thou* (A new translation, with a prologue and notes by Walter Kaufman). New York: Simon and Schuster, 1996.

Brian Cummings (Editor). *The Book of Common Prayer: The Texts of 1549, 1559, and 1662.* Oxford: Oxford University Press, 2011.

Ralph Waldo Emerson, *Essays and Lectures.* New York: Library of America, 1983.

Howard V. Hong; Edna H. Hong (Editors and Translators). *Søren Kierkegaard's Journals and Papers, Vol. I, A–E.* Bloomington: Indiana University Press, 1967.

Robert Hughes. *American Visions: The Epic History of Art in America.* New York: Alfred A. Knopf, 1997.

William James. *Writings 1902–1910.* New York: Library of America, 1987.

John Keats. *Selected Letters.* (John Barnard, Editor.) London: Penguin Books, 2014.

Iain McGilchrist. *The Master and His Emissary: The Divided Brain and the Making of the Western World.* New Haven and London: Yale University Press, 2009.

John Henry Newman. *Prayers, Verses and Devotions.* (With an introduction by Louis Bouyer.) San Francisco: Ignatius Press, 2019.

Louis Legrand Noble. *The Life and Works of Thomas Cole.* (Edited by Elliot S. Vesell.) Hensonville: Black Dome Press Corp., 1997.

Edgar Allan Poe. *The Complete Tales and Poems of Edgar Allan Poe.* London: Penguin Books, 1982.

Marshall B. Tymn (Compiler and Editor). *Thomas Cole's Poetry.* York: Liberty Cap Books, 1972.

Evelyn Underhill. *Mysticism: A Study in the Nature and Development of Man's Spiritual Consciousness.* New York: Meridian Books, 1956.

Evelyn Underhill (Editor). *The Cloud of Unknowing: The Classic of Medieval Mysticism.* Mineola: Dover Publications Inc., 2003.

Ludwig Wittgenstein. *Tractatus Logico-Philosophicus.* (D. F. Pears and B. F. McGuiness, Translators.) London and New York: Routledge, 1974.

Lin Yutang (Translator and Editor). *The Wisdom of Laotse.* New York: Random House, 1948.

www.ingramcontent.com/pod-product-compliance
Lightning Source LLC
LaVergne TN
LVHW060631110826
845147LV00014B/894

* 9 7 8 1 6 2 1 3 8 9 1 4 9 *